The Personal Life
of the Christian

The Personal Life of the Christian

ARTHUR W. ROBINSON

Formerly Vicar of
All Hallows Barking by the Tower

Oxford New York Toronto Melbourne

OXFORD UNIVERSITY PRESS

1980

Oxford University Press, Walton Street, Oxford OX2 6DP

London Glasgow New York Toronto
Delhi Bombay Calcutta Madras Karachi
Kuala Lumpur Singapore Hong Kong Tokyo
Nairobi Dar es Salaam Cape Town
Melbourne Wellington

and associated companies in
Beirut Berlin Ibadan Mexico City

© Preface J. A. T. Robinson 1981

First published by Longmans in 1902 under the title
The Personal Life of the Clergy

British Library Cataloguing in Publication Data

Robinson, Arthur William
    The Personal Life of the Christian.
    1. Christian Life—Anglican Authors
    I. Title
    248'.9'3   BV4501.2   80–40813
    ISBN 0-19-213427-2

Typeset by Hope Services, Abingdon
and printed in Great Britain by
Richard Clay & Co. Ltd., Bungay

A Grateful Foreword
by Bishop George Appleton

I still remember with gratitude a short course of Lenten addresses which Canon Arthur Robinson gave in 1924 when I was a student at St Augustine's College, Canterbury. The impression left on me through 50 years was of his great scholarship, deep devotion, and a desire for holiness. Shortly afterwards, the Warden of St Augustine's suggested that I might profit by reading Canon Robinson's book, written in 1902, on 'The Personal Life of the Clergy'. In the intervening years I must have read it through half a dozen times, and each time found it contemporary and compelling.

He said that he wrote at a time of great activity in church life when 'there is little time to read, or to think or to pray.' A later chapter headed 'Over-Occupation' drives home this message. Reading through his book again recently, I discovered that one of my most treasured quotations came from him: 'Prayer is work. Prayer is high work. Prayer is hard work. Prayer is our work'.

Another well remembered summary comes in his chapter on penitence: To sin against law is grievous, to sin against light is more grievous, but to sin against love is most grievous of all.

The chapter that captured me was entitled 'Devotion to our Lord', with its insistence that Christ is to be the object of supremest affection. He quotes from Liddon's *Bampton Lectures* a remarkable tribute to Jesus Christ from the Emperor Napoleon, written in his exile, 'When I saw men and spoke to them, I lighted up the flame of self-devotion in their hearts . . . Christ alone has succeeded in so raising the mind of man to the Unseen, that it becomes insensible to the barriers of time and space'.

Arthur Robinson would have felt that his son, John, was a chip off the old block, when towards the close of his courageous and challenging *Honest to God,* he quotes with convincing approval the closing words of Professor Herbert Butterfield's *Christianity and History:*

There are times when we can never meet the future with sufficient elasticity of mind, especially if we are locked in the contemporary systems of thought. We can do worse than remember a principle which both gives us a firm Rock and leaves us the maximum elasticity for our minds: the principle: Hold to Christ, and for the rest be totally uncommitted.

Arthur, too, with his urgent plea to his readers to go direct to the Gospels, the original sources of our knowledge of the Person of our Lord, would have rejoiced in John's *Can we Trust the New Testament?* It looks as if spiritual chromosomes are transmissible.

Epiphany 1980   GEORGE APPLETON

Contents

Preface

This book, by my father, Arthur William Robinson, was first published in 1902, under the title *The Personal Life of the Clergy*. It was his, characteristic, contribution to a series he edited for Longmans, *Handbooks for the Clergy*. Another volume, *The Study of the Gospels,* was written by his brother, Armitage Robinson, then Dean of Westminster.

I confess that it would not have occurred to me that pastoral theology of nearly eighty years ago—any more than that of the 1820s then!—would have stood reissuing today. But such was the recommendation in this instance to the Oxford University Press by Bishop George Appleton.

Coming from a man of such deep spirituality and wide sympathies, I knew it was a judgement that one must take seriously. So I have willingly co-operated with what seems to me a percipient and courageous publishing decision. For it was clear on reading the book through that it was remarkably unbound by the age to which it belonged. The number of changes that seemed necessary were few and superficial, and none of them touched the substance.

The main change has been in the title. For what relevance it has today goes a good deal wider than anything that affects the ranks of the professional clergy, now much reduced. Indeed, if we have learnt anything from the revolution in our theology of the Church and its ministry in recent years, it is surely that the distinctiveness of the priest lies not in his *difference from* the layman or in what the others *cannot* do—as if he could maintain his preserve only at their expense. His ministry is not, like that of the Old Testament priesthood, vicarious, but representative. His divine commission is to exercise in the name of the whole Body the ministry which belongs to every member and should therefore be shared by every member. As the servant of the servants of God, to use the proud title of the Pope, he is *par eminence* what all Christians are called to be. His spirituality therefore will be theirs, and the secret and power of his personal life a type for the entire priestly people in the world. As

Teilhard de Chardin put it, 'To the full extent of my power because I am a priest I wish from now on to be the *first* to become conscious of all that the world loves, pursues and suffers; I want to be the *first* to seek, to sympathize and to suffer; the *first* to open myself out and sacrifice myself—to become more widely human and more nobly of the earth than any of the world's servants'. And if this is the ideal, then at this interior level a handbook for the clergy should be able to serve *mutatis mutandis* as what Erasmus called an *Enchiridion Militis Christi*, a service manual for every Christian man and woman. But not everything in this book has been 'laicized'. Some of the specific references to the pastoral ministry have deliberately been allowed to stand. For they are still of relevance not only to clergy and ordinands but to the wider spectrum of those now being challenged to consider the role of priest-workers, as well as to laymen called increasingly to share and therefore to enter more deeply into the ministry of their clergy.

Naturally since 1902 many things have changed. Who could say today 'The word Duty is on all lips. We are proud of our pride in it'?! And the chapter on Depression could not now be written without more reference to purely psychological causes. But who also would have thought that secularization was already then a topic of theological discussion? Yet what makes a book date or fail to date cuts deeper and is more mysterious. The clue lies, I suspect, in whether even when it first appears it is secondhand or comes authentically from source. Is it, in the words of a parable in this book, 'the copy of a copy'? Or does it bear the marks of 'a freshness, a fearlessness, a freedom from conventionality, combined with a humility, a reverence, a patience, which . . . unmistakably betokens a character that has derived its impress and drawn its inspiration from . . . the Original'?

I never really knew my father—he died when I was nine—but through my mother, who lived to nearly ninety-six and was born a hundred years ago on the day I sign this, I recognize particularly in the 'humility, reverence and patience' of that description (though he would have been the first to disown it) something of a self-portrait. And it is this unmistakable timeless relation to source that gives, I believe, his words what lasting quality they possess—like those of another brother of that remarkable generation, Forbes Robinson, whose *Letters to his Friends* have become a spiritual classic of the twentieth century.

For those today who know nothing of the author, he was born, of Irish parentage, in 1856, the second of a family of eight sons and five daughters, most of whose lives evidenced the power of a very remarkable personal ministry. At the time my father wrote this book he was Vicar of All Hallows Barking by the Tower of London and Warden of the College of Mission Clergy instituted there by Archbishop Benson. In the course of this work, with which he was associated for nearly thirty years, he had unrivalled experience of conducting parish missions and clergy retreats not only at home but in Australia, New Zealand, South Africa and Canada. And it was out of this wealth and depth of experience that this and his other books were born, marked as they are by a deceptively simple profundity of spirit and an unsentimental natural wisdom. Though a D.D. of Cambridge and not long after this book a candidate for a Chair there, his depth of divinity was never paraded. During the first world war he was invited by Archbishop Davidson to lead the National Mission of Repentance and Hope and later appointed by him a Canon Residentiary of Canterbury—which is where I came upon the scene. I count it a humbling privilege after all this time to be asked in however small degree to repay and pass on the influence of that very personal life by which, largely unwittingly, I have been shaped.

29 December 1979   JOHN A.T. ROBINSON

Chapter 1

The Importance of the Subject

We are so constituted as naturally to wish for success. The wish
is a right and a noble one. It may, of course, like other right
and noble things, be sadly perverted and degraded. It may sink
into a vulgar desire for any sort of approbation, or for the even
less creditable satisfaction which too often accompanies material reward. But in its essential nature, and as originally im-
planted, it is by no means so poor a thing. Rather is it to be
likened to the longing for completeness and the yearning
after perfection which haunt and possess the soul of the artist;
may we not go even further and affirm that it is akin to the
delight which the supreme Creator takes in His work, and to
His determination that what He has made shall be 'very good'?

We wish to succeed. We have our ideals of what a lecture, a
sermon, a congregation, or a parish should be; and we cannot
easily rest until we have attained to something like the realization of our dream. We should not be better workmen, nor
should we be better men, were it otherwise with us.

We wish to succeed, and accordingly, when we see what looks
like success in the work of another, we are greatly attracted by
it, and are fired by the ambition to go and do what he has done.
We too would sway the multitude, would secure the confidence
of classes of people whom it is specially hard to win, would
gather about us a body of devout communicants and earnest,
intelligent workers. We too would make a lasting impression
for good upon the souls that are committed to our charge.

Alas! we know but too well that motives far short of the
highest may enter into such an ambition; yet, nevertheless, the
desire in itself—let us say it again—is a lawful and honourable
one. It is the wish to make full proof of our ministry, to be
workmen who have no need to be ashamed, to be in a position
to present without blemish 'the beautiful flock' which the

Chief Shepherd will one day require at our hands. He Himself, when speaking of the way in which His own earthly life had 'glorified' the Father who sent Him, knew the satisfaction of saying—'I have finished the work which Thou gavest Me to do.'

We have said that the sight of success is a thing that greatly attracts us. It is indeed pathetic to observe how those who appear to have achieved it are watched and questioned by their fellows who, as often as not, are much older men than themselves. What was it did it? where was the source of attractiveness? was there anything special in the methods employed? was it this? or was it that?

Even more pathetic is it to witness the attempts which are made to imitate the efforts and to reproduce the effects of others. For the most part, it goes almost without saying, they are made in vain. There is of course much, very much, to be learned from any one who has really succeeded in anything; but the learning must go far deeper than surface imitation. This is where so many lamentably fail. They set themselves to reproduce externals, plans and schemes; or possibly no more than manners, which at secondhand inevitably pass into mannerisms. Then, too, it is essential that we should keep in mind the elementary principle that no two of us were ever intended to be exactly alike; so that even were we to succeed in our endeavours to fashion ourselves after the pattern of somebody else, it could only be by the forfeiture of what was distinctive in ourselves, and as such a needed contribution to the life around us.

What, then, is the secret of influence? If it does not, as we have been saying, consist in a copying of what is most noticeable in the lives and practices of others, still less does it depend upon external conditions of station or wealth. Material resources may even be detrimental where it is a question of exerting the influence which is to do most for the upraising of men. It is recorded that Innocent IV and Thomas Aquinas were standing together as the bags of treasure were being carried in through the gates of the Lateran. 'You see,' observed the Pope with a smile, 'the day is past when the Church could say, "Silver and gold have I none"!' 'Yes, Holy Father,' was the saint's reply, 'and the day is past also when the Church could say to the lame man, "Rise and walk"!'

It is natural to imagine that intellectual gifts count for a great deal in the matter of such influence. Beyond question they do; and yet it is even more certain that they are not the chief factor, not even an indispensable factor. The most able and learned have not seldom been those who have most conspicuously failed.

Again, there can be no doubt that methods of organization may be made extremely effective. Yet it is often only too evident that these in themselves have a tendency to become fatally mechanical, until a condition of things may easily be reached in which the apparatus of machinery is kept going rather for its own sake than for any particular good that is expected to result from it.

But there is one illusion from which we find it most difficult of all to part. With our practical English temperament, we are always disposed to the belief that anything, or nearly anything, is to be accomplished by means of hard work. We are extremely slow to learn that, Work is not necessarily influence. Were it otherwise, this country of ours would be vastly more Christian than it is. At no time in its history was there more doing than at present. To go into a 'well-worked' parish, with its unceasing round of services, its multiplied agencies, its endless activities, is to a visitor fairly bewildering. As we turn the pages of the Church's 'Year Book' and read the records of meetings and societies, conferences and committees, involving perpetual discussions and hurryings to and fro, we almost marvel that in this little island we can still hear ourselves speak! Small wonder that from all sides there comes the complaint that the hours of the working day are too few, and that there is 'no time' to read, or to think, or to pray.

It is not meant to suggest that all these activities are fruitless, very far from it. All that is deprecated is the supposition—should we not rather say, the superstition?—that work is its own justification, and that simply to have got through so much of it is in itself a cause for congratulation. On the contrary, never did earnest workers need more than now to be brought face to face with the fact that it is possible to 'labour in vain,' to 'spend their strength for nought,' to toil day and night and yet take little or nothing.

The lesson of the true secret of influence, if we have learned it, was probably brought home to us in some such way as this. We had tried our experiments; we had gone on trying them for years. We had acted upon one plan after another, had adopted enthusiastically this suggestion and that, had spurred ourselves to constantly increasing efforts. And then, when the consciousness was deepening that we were as far from the secret as ever, it pleased God of His goodness, and He could scarcely have granted a greater boon, to send our way some simple soul whose every word seemed to tell, whose very presence carried a benediction; who, without our ability it may be, and with no special methods, evidently succeeded where we had most elaborately failed. The sight sent us to our knees to ask to be forgiven, and taught the way to begin from the very beginning again. What we had learnt was this. We had been made to realize that influence is the power that distils from a life that is lived in communion with God.

Shortly before his death, a former Lord Selborne paid a visit to Wales and addressed a gathering of churchmen there. It was at a time of much uncertainty, when many were anxiously wondering how the position of the Church in the principality was to be upheld. The speaker said a great deal that was wise, but there was one counsel which more than any other fixed itself in the memories of his hearers. 'Be spiritual'—he urged—'be spiritual, be spiritual.' That was the advice upon which he insisted most earnestly; and never in all his life did the great lawyer give truer counsel than that.

Thought and work are, after all, only the outcome and expression of life. It is by the quality of the life which underlies them that their character and worth is determined. Intellect is good, as an instrument is good; but intellect by itself is powerless. Organization is good, but only on the condition that, as in the prophet's vision, there are not merely 'wheels,' but also 'the Spirit within the wheels.' It is not what we say, not even what we do, but what we are, that tells. 'Do not speak to me,' said the American transcendentalist, with a pardonable exaggeration; 'what you are thunders so loud that

I cannot hear what you say!'

It would not be difficult to multiply illustrations and instances to show that to-day as of old 'the life is the light of men.'

A mission was being conducted in a pit village of the county of Durham. The schoolmaster of the place was a hard-headed north countryman; and it might have seemed that he was inclined to be somewhat hard-hearted too. At any rate, he had no great belief in missions, and did not think much of emotional religion. He was extremely reserved about the whole matter. But there was one topic upon which he was always ready to talk. Speak to him of a man who five-and-twenty years before had been the vicar of the district, and at once a chord was set vibrating within him. Asked one day whether he thought that his old vicar, who had become famous in the Church, was still the same humble and genuine man that he had been in the days when he had known him first, he replied at once in tones that were almost indignant; 'Why,' he said, 'you have only to shake that man's hand to feel that he is full of the Holy Ghost!' He could not have explained it, but he could quite well recognize the fact.

Not indeed that it has always been necessary to shake a man's hand before coming to a similar conclusion. An Archbishop of York told his Ordination candidates of a young clergyman who had been appointed to a country parish. His stay in it, as it proved, was not to be for long. He was scarcely more than thirty when he died. After an interval had passed, a friend who known him well visited the place, eager to discover what kind of impression he had made. Meeting a labourer, he asked him the question, 'Did he think Mr. — had done any good?' Again there was no sort of hesitation in the answer, 'I never saw that man cross the common yonder, sir, without being the better for it.'

Does it seem too high, too impossible an aim, that the people should be the better for the simple fact of our presence among them, and that even our slightest actions should speak to them of good? Can we really be satisfied with any conception of our mission and responsibility less than that? Is not the life of the priest and Christian intended to be a sort of sacrament to their people? Should they not be able to see in it 'an outward and visible sign of an inward and spiritual grace,' a 'pledge' which will assure them of the reality of that which is beyond merely natural powers, and a 'means' whereby they are to be encouraged and helped to attain it?

Whether we think so or not, men do take knowledge of us. They are well able to perceive it when we are in a low state of spiritual vitality, and they seldom fail to be aware of the fact when our inner life is healthy and strong.

Are we then saying too much when we say, and say decidedly, that the consideration of our personal lives must of necessity be set in the forefront of any attempts to increase the efficiency of our work; and that all other considerations must be regarded as subordinate to this one?

The treatment of such a subject is a matter of peculiar delicacy and difficulty. In many ways what is to be said will fall, perhaps must inevitably fall, far short of what both writer and readers could wish. It is, however, permissible to believe that it will not be without its use if it should have the effect of convincing any one of us of the necessity of going into the whole question much more thoroughly for himself. It certainly will not be in vain, if it should lead us to cast ourselves more humbly upon that higher wisdom which is ever most ready to help us just at the point at which we have honestly tried, and failed, to help one another.

Note I

The following passages occur in an address by Archbishop Benson, on 'Spiritual Power', which formed part of his Third Visitation Charge:[1]

If we look to Scripture we find the word 'Power' used almost indiscriminately in the Authorised Version to render two very different words, 'Εξουσία 'authority' (externally conferred power), and Δύναμις 'potency,' 'ability' to which our usage of 'power' more properly belongs.

Both ought to co-exist in the Church. Our Lord taught and worked with 'authority' as well as with 'power,' and the Apostles received 'power' as well as 'authority,' and the Christian clerus ought to have both. But they may be separated in the Church. The Scribes and Pharisees 'knew not the power of God,' but they still 'sate in Moses' seat' and their 'authority' was to be attended to. In the Church of Israel

[1] See *Fishers of Men*, pp. 110 ff.

when the priesthood ceased, the prophets had 'power' but no levitical 'authority.'

And so history shows how in sinful times 'power' has departed from 'authority' and has reappeared in enthusiasms, in separations, in alienated communities not to be reunited till their crisis comes. And fearlessly we must say that terrible as is the putting asunder of what God hath joined together, yet 'power' without 'authority' is a more living thing, a more saving thing, than 'authority' without power . . . .

What so hollow as for authority to have to vindicate itself conscious of departed power? But alas! the man feels it must be done, and so does an institution . . . Thus, failing the power, a working substitute for it is provided. The authority remains, it must act; if its inner force flags a little it must be propped up. There is no original intention to deceive: rather to keep up the standard when the heart sank. Gradually the service of religion is mechanized, and even then it is so soothing and so fair, as it gently becomes more material and sensuous, that it is delighted in. It is even a kind of conscientiousness which searches for working substitutes when the acquisition and exercise of that real spiritual power which lies in the awful contact with Christ's holiness and judgment is too painful and constant.

Note II

Speaking to those engaged in teaching at the universities and in public schools, Bishop Paget said:

'For their sakes I consecrate myself.' There is the ultimate secret of power; the one sure way of doing good in our generation. We cannot anticipate or analyse the power of a pure and holy life; but there can be no doubt about its reality, and there seems no limit to its range. We can only know in part the laws and forces of the spiritual world; and it may be that every soul that is purified and given up to God and to His work releases or awakens energies of which we have no suspicion—energies viewless as the wind; but we can can be sure of the result, and we may have glimpses sometimes of the process.

Surely, there is no power in the world so unerring or so irrepressible as the power of personal holiness. All else at times goes wrong, blunders, loses proportion, falls disastrously short of its aim, grows stiff or one-sided, or out of date— 'whether there be prophecies, they shall fail; whether there be tongues, they shall cease; whether there be knowledge, it shall vanish away'; but nothing mars or misleads the influence that issues from a pure and humble and unselfish character.

A man's gifts may lack opportunity, his efforts may be misunderstood and resisted; but the spiritual power of a consecrated will needs no opportunity, and can enter where the doors are shut. By no fault of a man's own, his gifts may suggest to some the thoughts of criticism, comparison, competition; his self-consecration can do no harm in this way. Of gifts, some are best for long distances, some for objects close at hand or in direct contact; but personal holiness, determining, refining, characterizing everything that a man says and does, will tell alike on those he may not know even by name, and on those who see him in the constant intimacy of his home.

—*The Hallowing of Work,* pp. 16 f.

Chapter 2

Our Part and Duty in the Matter

In what is to be written in these pages no apology will be offered for simplicity of style or directness of statement. Things will be said with which we are all of us perfectly familiar, and which we are constantly saying to others. The fact that they are thus familiar and often on our lips is not a reason for omitting them here; it is rather a reason why we should be asked to consider them the more carefully, and apply them to ourselves.

It is no mere paradox to assert that we all of us, clergy and lay-people alike, most need to learn the things which we have known the longest. And who is likely to urge them upon us of the clergy, if we do not urge them on ourselves? It may encourage us to remember how freshly familiar truths can appear when we bring ourselves to view them from the standpoint of our particular needs and hopes. No things after all are really so 'new' as the things which are both 'new and old.'

In this chapter we shall consider, and try to lay to heart, a most elementary lesson. So elementary is it that we are in serious danger of neglecting it altogether. The lesson is this, that, what we are to be must in great measure depend upon the efforts we are prepared to make. If we are to become more spiritual men, it can only be because we are firmly determined that it shall be so.

We cannot assert this principle with too much emphasis, nor can we make too sure of the foundation upon which the assertion rests.

To begin with, let us dismiss the fear that there is any inconsistency between what we shall now say and what has been said already. In the preceding chapter we had occasion to maintain very strongly that failure must inevitably result when 'work' is made a substitute for the influence which can only flow from spirituality of life. It might therefore at first sight look as if we were now going to restore the thought of work to the position of primary importance from which we had hitherto been trying to dislodge it. But indeed it is not so. There is no sort of inconsistency in saying, on the one hand, that effort is no substitute for grace; and on the other, that grace demands from us the most untiring co-operation of effort.

If we are teaching rightly, we are perpetually insisting upon both these truths. We tell our hearers that the duties to which they are pledged by their Christian profession are such as they cannot hope to perform in their own strength, and that they must be continually dependent upon a higher power. At the same time we tell them that this power can never be theirs against their will; that God's help is in fact only given to those who will help themselves.

It is no small part of our message to make men see that it is ever God's way to treat them with respect. Wonderful as it is, He asks our leave to bless us. As we do not think of entering the dwelling of another until we have obtained his permission, even so the heavenly visitor says of Himself, 'I stand at the door and knock.' Everything must depend upon our readiness to allow the Divine power to have free course in our hearts and lives.

That, then, which we teach to others we must also teach ourselves. It may help to make the lesson real to us if we reflect how thoroughly of a piece are God's dealings with the whole of His creation, so far as we have knowledge of them.

In an early Christian document, the so-called *Epistle to Diognetus,* there is a memorable sentence which deserves to be written in letters of gold—'Force is not an attribute of God' (§7). A little consideration is enough to enable us to see how universal the application of this great law of liberty is.

The supreme distinction between ourselves and the creatures beneath us lies in the fact that, whereas they obey involuntarily, without any clear consciousness of what obedience means, the service expected from us is a service of deliberate choice.

> If thou would'st attain thy highest, go look on a flower;
> What it does will-lessly, do thou willingly.[1]

The flower is for ever doing; opening its petals to welcome the influences of heaven, gathering through roots and leaves the elements which contribute to its upbuilding, yielding always to the laws of its being. Even so, in like manner, is it for the man to strive and mount upwards towards the fulfilment of his ideal.

True it is that in God 'we live and move and have our being,' and that without Him we 'can do nothing.' The new birth is His act. Christian character is His creation. All its beauty, all its fragrance, are a witness to His presence in the soul. Yet it is not less true that Christian character is the result of human endeavour. The Christian is not only born but made. It is our part, our necessary part, to 'work out' that which God is working in us. It is for us to 'labour striving according to His working which worketh in us mightily.'

God, we believe, never enforces; but He is ever waiting to enable. 'Force is not an attribute of God'; but, 'Twice I have also heard the same, that power belongeth unto God.'[2] And God's power becomes ours as we accept and obey it.

That progress in the spiritual life has been made to depend upon our efforts appears even more convincingly to be part of the great order under which we live, when we pass from the merely physical sphere to the intellectual, and take our illustrations from facts and experiences connected with mental proficiency which no one would think of disputing. In this connection, as it may be well to be reminded, we are constantly employing expressions which we have borrowed, in the sense in which we employ them, from religion. We speak, that is to say, of 'gifts,' and of 'talents,' and of 'endowments,' which belong to us, if they are ours at all, as part of our heritage. We have powers and faculties which we did not originate in ourselves. But the recognition of this fact does not lead us to imagine that we have no responsibility in regard to them. We know quite well that we must cultivate them diligently, if they are to avail us anything. Otherwise the failure will be great in proportion to the opportunity.

[1] Schiller.   [2] Ps. 62:11.

Gifts do not relieve their possessors from the necessity of hard work. 'Genius,' in the oft-quoted definition, 'is an infinite capacity for taking pains.' It is the merest delusion to suppose that anything really great has ever been achieved without effort. True no doubt it is in a sense that 'every man does his best thing easiest'; but unremitting has been the toil which has gained for him the facility. And the result, when it comes, is rightly described as a 'work' of genius.

Those who have had the best right to speak have been unanimous in their testimony that nothing really worthy of attainment, in art, or in literature, or in science, is to be reached without labour—continuous, systematic labour. True again it is in a most real sense that the 'yoke is easy' and the 'burden is light,' for the task is congenial and the reward is not wanting; but the stoop of the back and the furrows on the brow make it evident that there is a yoke to be carried and a burden to be borne.

When someone inquired of Sir Joshua Reynolds how long it had taken him to paint a certain picture, he answered, 'All my life.'

'If I omit one day's practice,' so Rubinstein is reported to have said, 'I know it the next day, the critics know it the day after, and the public the day after that.'

When Dr Liddon was asked to give some lectures to younger men about preaching, he refused, declaring that he 'could only tell them to take pains.'

'If the scholar feels reproach when he reads the tale of the extreme toil and endurance of the Arctic explorer, he is not working as he should.'[1]

If then it be true that

> The heights by great men gained and kept,
> Were not attained by sudden flight;
> But they while their companions slept,
> Were toiling upwards through the night,

how is it to be supposed that it can be otherwise with great saints? If it takes years of practice to perfect a musician, how much practice must it not take to perfect a Christian? Will eight

[1] *Emerson in Concord*, p. 219.

hours a day do it? Nay, those who have longed the most to attain proficiency in the highest art of holy living have not been content with so little. Their prayer has been that every moment of conscious, and indeed of half conscious existence, might be devoted to the task. They have desired that even in their dreams they might be nearer and still nearer to heaven. Of one, who was remarkable for self-control and a singular sweetness of disposition, it was said that he 'took infinite pains with himself.'

Yet it is by no means uncommon to hear language which is calculated to leave the impression that all that is required in order to produce the highest type of Christian excellence is a fuller operation of Divine grace. There is a sense in which this is undeniably true; but it may be most dangerously false if what is intended is that there is no immediate need for any action of our own. Let us not be deceived by what may appear to be good words. They may not be the less misleading because they assume a look of humility. Let us not presume to cast the blame of our own shortcomings upon God. If He is straitened, we may be sure that it is not in Himself, but in us. He gives grace freely; but it cannot be given where it is certain that it will be received in vain.

Shall we say then that grace is 'an infinite capacity for taking pains'? St Paul would not have quarrelled with that definition. Indeed it seems to underlie his own confession, when he says: 'By the grace of God I am what I am; and His grace which was bestowed upon me was not in vain; but I laboured more abundantly than they all.'[1]

Might we not go a step further, and say what may seem an even bolder thing? Might we not dare to assert that a gift of more grace would not make life easier for us, but harder? The presence of genius, as we have seen, does not absolve men from the necessity of toil. Nay rather, it is this very presence which more than anything else binds and pledges them to spend laborious days; which assigns them to the task of surmounting the most formidable difficulties. Even so, it would appear, does the presence of grace pledge us to labour upon labour. 'For this very cause' we are bound to give all diligence that we

[1] 1 Cor. 15:10.

may add virtue to virtue in our endeavour to 'press toward the mark for the prize of the high calling,' and to 'apprehend' that for which we were 'apprehended of Christ Jesus.'[1]

If we are to grow in grace, then, let us be assured that we have our part to do. If we are to receive the 'more life and fuller,' we must open our hearts to welcome and bend our wills to obey. If we desire a place in the 'kingdom,' we must prepare to hear the challenge, 'Can ye drink of the cup?' 'Can ye be baptized with the baptism?' If we long to exercise influence for the blessing of others, we must be ready to sanctify ourselves for their sakes, and must not count it strange that in the process there is much to endure.

Happy for us if the lesson has been learned at the outset of our ministerial life. A young clergyman had called to see Bishop Benson at Truro. At the close of the interview, the bishop passed across the table a sheet of paper on which he had written the concluding sentence of the first book of *The Imitation of Christ* by Thomas à Kempis: 'Tantum proficies, quantum tibi ipsi vim intuleris.' Take that for your motto, he said.

Let us settle it in our minds, whether early or late, that if we are not advancing in spirituality of life, the fault is to be sought within. We can only make progress as we bring pressure to bear upon ourselves. It is 'through faith and patience'— 'faith', which gratefully traces all good gifts to their source in God, and 'patience', which as gladly accepts and bravely fulfils the conditions upon which we can use them with profit— that we, like those before us, may hope to 'inherit the promises'.

NOTE

It is strange how slow we are to lay hold of some of the most elementary principles of spiritual life. Nothing, for example, seems to many of us to be harder to grasp than the fact of the utility of effort when rightly made in harmony with the Divine intention. We make efforts, right efforts, and they appear to fail; our good resolutions come, as we imagine, to nothing. Then we lose heart, and are inclined to abandon endeavour. It is, we say, 'no use trying'. The insufficiency of such reasoning we should

[1] 2 Pet. 1:5; Phil. 3:12, 14.

see without difficulty if we were to put an analogous case in the sphere of more ordinary education. A child, let us say, has been practising a music lesson. He has worked hard, but when the master comes, the result is absolute failure. The child is discouraged and perplexed, and declares that he will try no more. Accordingly for the next lesson he makes no preparation, but nevertheless he does remarkably well. And now his conclusion is triumphant: 'When I tried the hardest I did the worst; and when I didn't try at all I got on best'! For us the child's logic serves but to raise a smile. We see, of course, that the final success was due to the previous work. At the moment the work did not tell, probably on account of excitement or self-consciousness which upset the nervous balance; but in the end the effect became apparent.

Is it not a similar conclusion that we ought to draw for ourselves when we have tried most, prayed most, struggled most, and seem to have overcome the least? It may really have been so, for the moment; but we think that, on that account, the effort expended has been labour lost. There is such a thing as the conservation of spiritual energy. The result will most certainly appear, perhaps when we are entirely unconscious of the cause to which it is to be traced. No effort, no aspiration, no genuine attempt at self-discipline, is ever thrown away. 'In due season we shall reap, if we faint not.'

'My brethren,' said Richard Baxter at the close of a sermon, 'I have given you an easy lesson, hard to learn.' There are in religion many easy lessons hard to learn. This is one of them; we shall have others to note as we proceed.

Chapter 3

The Need of Penitence

Once we have firmly laid hold of the thought that it is essential to our progress that we should use all diligence in order that the grace which is given to us may not be received in vain, it becomes our wisdom to go on to ask how in particular we are to set about the task of self-discipline. No acceptance of general principles, however true, can be enough for our purpose; indeed, as we must be aware, general resolutions do not as a rule lead to much. What then, we must inquire, are the directions in which we are especially bound to put forth endeavour? Where is it that we are likely to be weakest and most at fault? The answer to these questions may well differ for different men, as they must certainly differ for different times. All we can attempt is to indicate what will be the true answers for many of us, possibly for most of us, at the present time.

Those who, by their work as missioners or conductors of retreats, are brought into closest relations with the personal experience of their fellows, would probably not hesitate long if called upon to upon to say what they believed to be the greatest need in the religious life of to-day. They would say that it is the need for a deeper penitence.

Nor would this testimony be confined to the clergy. Mr Gladstone once wrote an article in which he dealt with certain theological difficulties then much discussed in connection with a widely circulated work of fiction. The most remarkable thing in that article was the assertion of the writer's conviction that the great majority of all such difficulties have their origin in an inadequate sense of sin.

In a conversation with a friend, reported in print soon after his death, the same great Church layman went even further and declared most deliberately that in his opinion this absence of a due sense of sin was 'the great want in modern life.' ' "Ah," said he slowly, "the sense of sin—that is the great want in modern life; it is wanting in our sermons, wanting everywhere!" This was said slowly and reflectively, almost like a monologue.'[1]

Perhaps the most effective way of making ourselves realize the extent of the need is to contrast the condition of things familiar to us now with the state of religious teaching and feeling in days not very far removed in the past.

We are accustomed to set over against each other the main characteristics of the Evangelical High Church and schools of religious thought. We find no difficulty in describing the differences which distinguished the one from the other—differences of standpoint, of aim, and of method. It might be wished that we were equally accustomed to take note of the points which, in spite of these differences, they firmly maintained in common. Among such agreements we shall find that none was more marked than the entire unanimity with which the teachers of both schools insisted upon the absolute necessity of a true appreciation of the nature and guilt of sin. The language in which the teaching was conveyed might differ, but the meaning and intention were the same.

The Evangelicals were determined that none who came under their influence should be left in any doubt about the matter. They instructed their converts at the outset as to the need for repentance. They never wearied of speaking about 'conviction' of sin, and the 'burden' of sin, and the 'corruption' of human nature, and its 'fallen condition' in the sight of a holy God. And these were much more than phrases to them: they were stern and tremendous realities. Their meaning had been learnt by actual and painful experiences. These were the subject of their sermons and of their hymns. We have the confidential records of them in their letters, and in the diaries which they blotted with their tears.

Nor was it otherwise with the teachers of the opposite school, unless indeed it might be maintained that these were even more precise and systematic in their dealings with the matter. What they aimed at perpetually was to 'deepen penitence', to lead to a truer 'contrition'. They spared no effort, and they shrank from no process of personal humiliation. Self-

[1] *Talks with Mr Gladstone*, by the Hon. L. A. Tollemache, p. 96.

examination with them was raised into a science. They scrutinized motives as under a microscope, and by a particular 'confession,' not merely of sin but of sins, they sought to lead themselves and their penitents to an ever-increasing apprehension of their need of pardon and grace.

The essential conviction was one and the same with them both; indeed, at times the very language in which it was expressed was identical. Passages from the writings of Simeon and of Pusey have been set side by side; and so much alike are they that it would not be possible, from internal evidence alone, to tell from which they had come.[1]

From such a retrospect we turn our eyes to religion as we know it now. We mark its activities, its ever widening range of social interests, its larger outlook upon historical and scientific inquiry, its more accurate exegesis. There is so much that is useful and good. We are thankful for the advance that has been made in so many directions. And yet, if it be true that we are losing our penitence, there is need to pause and consider. What if it should prove that the foundations upon which we are building are insecurely laid? And what if the building itself be of less consequence than we have been inclined to suppose?

Those who went before us did go deep, and they did train saints. The fruit of their work was to be seen in men and women who were humble and unworldly in their aims, who genuinely cared for souls, who took delight in their religion, and made the reality of it felt in their lives. And it is impossible not to connect these effects with the profound self-knowledge, the trembling sense of personal unworthiness, which teachers and taught alike earnestly declared to have been at the basis of them. If we have changed all that, we have need to reflect very seriously both as to our present condition and our future prospects.

Perhaps the best hope for us lies in the fact that we are for the most part quite ready to admit that there has been this change, perplexed though we may be to know how to account for it, or to deal with the situation to which it has given rise.

This certainly is not the place in which to attempt any-

[1] See Liddon's *Life* of Pusey, vol. iii. pp. 96, 98.

thing like a complete investigation into the influences which
have been at work to lessen for us the sense of the seriousness
of sin. It must be enough if, by way of suggestion, we can
indicate some of the chief of them.

The most evident has been the force of reaction. There was
a sternness, we might even say a severity, about the older
teaching and its ways. Truths were set forth in statements
which were repellent to many minds. At the same time the
outward arrangements of worship were too often slovenly and
dull. The recoil from this state of things led to a determination
to make religion attractive at almost any cost. The winning
aspects of it were to be continually presented. On all sides
it was insisted that services should be 'bright': until not a
few of us have grown heartily tired of the word, and would
gladly restore somewhat of the old solemnity and wholesome
restraint.

But of course we shall have to go deeper than this if we are
to discover the fundamental causes of the change of which we
are thinking. When we do penetrate beneath the surface we
quickly find ourselves in the presence of a cause which is as
fundamental as any could be. This is nothing less radical than
an entirely altered conception of the character of God as shown
in His relations with men.

To the teachers who preceded us the dominant conception
of theology was, without question, that of the moral government of God. They took the thought from those who had gone
before them. We recall the phrase as occurring perpetually in
the writings of Bishop Butler.[1] The idea was uppermost in the
minds of most of those who thought seriously in the century
that followed him, whether they were philosophers, or divines,
or evangelists. They all made that conception the starting-
point of their thinking, and they never allowed themselves to
lose sight of it. The Divine attributes upon which they dwelt
and insisted were such as were most directly connected with it.
They spoke much of justice, and will, and power to administer
punishment. To them the true human attitude was an attitude
of submission and obedience. All else was revolt, such as would

[1] It is related of this great bishop that in his last solemn moments he 'expressed
it as an awful thing to appear before the Moral Governor of the world.'

inevitably draw upon itself the penalties of a broken law. To these thinkers it was therefore natural to give great prominence to the prospect of judgment, and to the disgrace and guilt of sin.

We have but to bring before our minds such an outline of the religious position, as it existed at a time well within living memory, in order to heighten our consciousness of the extraordinary revolution that has occurred in our modern theological thinking.

There may be exaggeration in the story as it is sometimes told, how a statesman, having been struck by a phrase as it fell from the lips of a preacher, repeated it during the course of a speech in his place in the House of Commons, only to discover that others were as ready to grasp at it as he himself had been. The phrase was—'the Fatherhood of God'. What is certain is that the truth when it came seemed new. To most it was a surprise: to many it was a revelation. It rapidly passed from lip to lip, it found its way into books, it took possession of hearts. Men believed it passionately. They came prepared to listen to those, and to those only, who would develop it for them. Their English reverence for the sanctities of the home made them ready to receive it. They found it in the Gospels. They saw that it underlay the great prayer of their childhood. Before long the demand became general for a theology which should be entirely expressed in the terms of this single truth.

Now we need not hesitate for an instant to express our deep thankfulness for all that we have gained in the course of this transition. We could scarcely over-estimate the debt that we owe to those through whom it has been effected. We have such cause to be grateful as men have for sunshine and summer heat. There has come to multitudes a fresh unveiling of light and love. Never in the history of Christendom were more people more intelligently able to pronounce the first great sentence of the Creed—'I believe in God the Father Almighty.' A wholly new significance has been given to the message of the Incarnation of the Son; fresh and unlooked-for help has been found by many who, under the older teaching, had been sorely perplexed by the doctrine of Christian Regeneration. And we might easily lengthen our list of such benefits.

At the same time it requires little effort to enable us to see that so marked a change of standpoint would be likely to make a very real difference to the consideration of such subjects as the certainty of judgment and the sinfulness of sin.

Nor is it difficult to understand how, as time went on and the new ideas more completely took the place of the old, the effect upon the popular religion would become increasingly noticeable. As an exclusive insistence upon the 'moral government' had produced a sternness and asperity from which the religious instinct in men might rightly welcome relief; so, too, an exclusive insistence upon the 'Fatherhood' would tend to produce results which in their turn might prove to be even more unsatisfactory. Fatherliness dissociated from firmness may for a while be attractive as a doctrine, but it can only lead to a laxity alike of thought and of practice. Happily, in the long run, it must cease to be popular, because it must cease to be believable. Love is never more terribly wronged and degraded than when represented as merely good-nature. Such a travesty can retain no lasting hold on mind, or heart, or conscience.

We are so much accustomed to dwell upon the gains which modern theology has owed to modern science, that we are probably inclined to overlook the fact that there have been some very real, even if only temporary, losses as well. Thus, for example, it will scarcely be questioned that the scientific doctrine of evolution, greatly as it has aided us in attaining to a more intelligent appreciation of the history of the training of the race, and greatly as it has strengthened the foundation upon which we rest our hopes for the future, has also done not a little to weaken the general sense of the seriousness of sin, by seeming to encourage the notion that evil may after all be but a stage, and a necessary stage, in the development of good; a notion from which it is easy to pass on to the denial that we can have any real responsibility in the matter.

So also, for our generation at all events, the gain from the influence of science upon religious thought has been seriously counterbalanced by a widespread weakening of the meaning of law. The word is on all lips; every one is talking of the operation of law, of the reign of law, of obedience to law. But the word, when we test it, weighs lighter than it did. Owing to its constant employment in reference to the material sphere, it has for multitudes ceased to bear any moral signification at all. From the old meaning of the authority of a superior will, it has come to denote no more than inevitable sequence. Here again, then, we recognize one among the influences which have tended to lessen the sense of moral responsibility which was once firmly established in the general religious mind.

To these more important causes we may add others which are none the less real because we cannot dignify them by the epithets 'theological' or 'scientific'. If we are to be perfectly candid, we shall have to admit that the condition of things which we are trying to account for is to be traced in no small degree to a habit of mind but little removed from indolence. On all hands the demand is being made for the minimizing of labour in every possible way. Nor is the shrinking from sustained exertion only to be observed in the region of manual work. It is equally apparent in the region of the intellect. Those who are best qualified to judge are continually warning us that our age is one of diffusion rather than depth. There is much information, with little understanding. Everything is being made easy. We have popular lectures which give us in an agreeable form the results of the studies of others. Leading articles are cut up into sections, with headlines to indicate their purport; while newspapers are filled with pictures so as to save us still further the effort of thinking.

We must not wonder if the same tendencies make themselves felt in the highest and most difficult sphere. We want to be good, but with the least possible trouble. Speak of the importance of definite belief, or of the value of self-discipline and mortification of the flesh, urge the necessity of living by rule—and to many you will appear as some belated survival of a less enlightened age. We flatter ourselves that at last, thanks to modern improvements, we have got 'reading without tears'; and we can see no reason why we should not have 'religion without tears' as well! And, indeed, we have plenty of it. But what is its worth? how deep does it go, or how high? has it joy, has it peace? what is its vision? and what is its power of influence?

It is when we ask questions like these that we see why it is that, although we have reason to be grateful for real gains which have come to us in recent years, we have yet little cause to be satisfied with the general result. We certainly cannot be content with the new, so long as we miss the solemnity, the strength, the spirituality of the old.

Enough then, by way of suggestion, as to the influences which have operated to weaken our sense of the meaning of sin: enough at all events to guide us in regard to the directions in which we may look, and must work, for a remedy.

Shall we not hope, for instance, that there may be a reaction from the reaction? that without necessarily returning to the former extreme of harshness, we may at least come to an agreement that 'the fear of the Lord is the beginning of wisdom', that reverence is the atmosphere in which alone the life of the soul can grow, and that the religion which stirs the emotions but fails to arouse the conscience is a sadly defective religion?

If this is to be, we must have a stronger preaching and teaching than has been common of late. There must be a more definite invoking of the Holy Spirit, whose office it is to convince of sin. And we must not shun to declare 'the whole counsel' of God, as set forth by our Lord and His Apostles. What is especially needed is the fuller theology which will harmonize the two conceptions of the character of God: which will shew us the 'Father of our spirits' as at the same time the 'Judge of all the earth'; which, when it leads us to address Him, will teach us to say 'Our Father, Which art in heaven, Hallowed be Thy name'; and to add with an equal fervour of conviction, 'Thy kingdom come, Thy will be done'.

We must proclaim, as Christ did, the great principles of the 'Father's kingdom'; and must show that love is not only compatible with, but inconceivable apart from, the wrath which is 'revealed from heaven against all ungodliness and unrighteousness of men'. People must be made to feel that 'the New Testament is a severe book',[1] and to see that the aim of its teaching is nothing less than salvation from sin. The Cross

[1] Dean Church.

must be set forth not only as 'the mirror of the love of God', but also as the measure of the guilt of man.

Then too we have need to school ourselves afresh to speak about the Judgment Day. It will not be an easy task, in the existing mood of feeling, to treat this momentous theme in such a way as to carry conviction to the understanding and the conscience. We must find out how to do it.

It may perhaps be worth while to relate an incident from the experience of one amongst us, as an instance of how the attempt may be made. He had been summoned to what proved to be the deathbed of a man in the parish in which he was serving. The man was a sculptor of no small pretensions: some of his figures are to be seen on the west front of one of our cathedrals. He was evidently very ill. The good priest could not but ask him how far he was prepared for the great change if it came. The reply was of the kind we have heard so often. He did not know that he had any particular reason to fear; he had done his best, and could think of many who had not succeeded as well.

We recognize the type, and we are well aware of the difficulty of making much impression upon it. The clergyman was silent for a few moments. Then what he said was this:

'Suppose I were to take a block of your stone, and a mallet, and one of your chisels; and were to set to work to carve out a head like one of those in your studio. I should do my best, and the result might be better than I had expected; and my friends might say that they had no idea that I had it in me to do anything of the kind: until I really began to be quite pleased with my work. But what if I brought it to you? You would wish to be kind, but you would see at a glance that there was nothing to praise. You might tell me that, with years of labour and training, I might possibly make a tolerable sculptor; but you would know well enough that what I had accomplished so far was simply nothing at all; that there was no sort of merit or distinction about it, that, in fact, the stone had been ruined and wasted. And why would you judge so? Why, of course, because you would look at the matter with an artist's eye; you would measure the work by the standard of your ideal of what it should have been, and you would therefore be able to estimate the extent of the failure.'

Then he went on to point out the application of the parable. We men take our lives into our own hands, and set about to fashion them according to our own notions of what they should be. We imagine that we have succeeded fairly enough, and we are assured that it would be well for society if more of the lives about us were as good. But the time will come when we must appear before God for His judgment: and what will that be? He, the great Artist, has had His ideal for each one of us. He would have shown it to us, and have realized it in us, if we had been willing to be taught and directed. As it is, our efforts are too often made in direct opposition to His purposes. He can judge us only by the extent to which His ideal has been attained. Much, therefore, that may seem respectable to us, must appear as the most lamentable failure in His eyes.

The man listened attentively, and candidly admitted that this way of looking at the matter did 'make a difference'. It was a new light, because it shewed him his actions in their relation to the Divine intention, about which he had never taken a thought.

Only as we can help people to believe that God has a high intent for each one of us, and that to defeat this is to disappoint Him and to inflict a grievous wrong upon ourselves, shall we be able to deliver them from the easy-going creed which encourages them to imagine that, because they are in the hands of goodness, it can matter little what they do, or leave undone. Our teaching will not have accomplished what it should until it has produced a keen conviction that to sin against *law* is grievous, to sin against *light* is more grievous, but to sin against *love* is most grievous of all.[1]

Then also we shall do well to lay greater stress than many of us have been wont to lay, upon the gracious ordering whereby a supernatural gladness flows forth as the effect of forgiveness into the truly repentant heart. There is no joy on earth which can exceed it. We must sing the praises of repentance, 'that stoop of the soul which in bending upraises it too'. The tear-

---

[1] See Bishop Walsham How, *The Closed Door*, p. 96.

drop lens has been to many a one the gate of pearl through which he has caught his first real glimpses of the kingdom drawing nigh.

But—and it is to this that all our consideration has been leading us—there is an indispensable condition apart from which we can hope to do little or nothing. The Christian must be the penitent. It is for him to lead the way. He more than others must feel the need and make the effort. The true theology which we proclaim must first have been preached to ourselves. We must bend low before the Cross; and we must ever act as those who are to be manifested before the Judgment Seat. Ours must be the blessedness of pardon; and ours the 'sorrow for forgiven sin'.

We have but to think of the interval that divides the utterances of the fifth and the sixth chapters of the book of Isaiah, in order to realize how different in their effects may be the teachings of the same teacher in regard to sin. The continuous 'woe' of chapter 5 is tremendous, and it might seem as if nothing could stand against it; yet who of us does not feel that he has pssed into another atmosphere, charged with an altogether different power to move and to melt, when in chapter 6 the same speaker is heard to exclaim, 'Woe is *me* for I am undone'?

Denunciations of evil are strangely unavailing. Our pulpits might ring with them, and our hearers be no better. But the pleading of the man who speaks of sins as he only can speak, who has felt the uncleanness and shame of them in his own soul, appeals with a power such as no force of words can give.

Never were people more ready to detect unreality in a preacher than those to whom we minister to-day: and never do they more quickly perceive it than when the subject is the subject of sin. If we are to convince them we must before all else be sincere. If we are not, we had better be silent until we can speak what we know. Then we may not always succeed; till then we shall certainly fail.

Note

(From the Private Devotions of Bishop Andrewes)

THE AGGRAVATION OF SIN

Its measure,
    its harm,
    its scandal.
Its quality,
Its iteration,—how often?
Its continuation,—how long?
The person,—by whom?
    his age, condition, state, enlightenment.
Its manner,
Its motive,
Its time,
Its place,
Its folly, ingratitude, hardness, contempt.

AN ACT OF CONFESSION

O God, Thou knowest my foolishness,
    and my sins are not hid from Thee,
      I also acknowledge them,
and my sin is ever before me.

Lord, Thou knowest all my desire,
    and my groaning is not hid from Thee.
Thou knowest, Lord, that I speak the truth
      in Christ, and lie not;
    my conscience also bearing me witness
      in the Holy Ghost,
    that I have great heaviness and continual
      sorrow in my heart,
    because I have thus sinned against Thee;
that I am a burden to myself in that I cannot
      sorrow more;
    that I beseech from Thee
      a contrite heart.

    Woe is me!
That I did not reverence nor dread
the incomprehensibleness of Thy Glory,
    Thy tremendous Power,
    the awfulness of Thy Presence,

Thy strict Justice,
Thy lovable Goodness.

And now, O Lord, humbling myself
    under Thy mighty hand,
for Thy great mercy, and for the glory of Thy Name,
    be merciful unto my sin:
for it is great; for it is exceeding great.
For the multitude, the great multitude,
    of thy loving-kindnesses,
Lord, O Lord, be merciful unto me, of
    sinners the greatest.

O my Lord, where sin hath abounded,
there let Grace more exceedingly abound,
    O Lord, hear; O Lord, forgive;
      O Lord, hearken and do;
defer not for Thine own sake, O my God.

Chapter 4

The Difficulty of Prayer

Bishop John Selwyn used to tell that, as his father, the first Bishop of New Zealand, was one day sitting in his study in Norfolk Island, a knock was heard at the door. A head looked in, which was at once recognized as that of a catechist from a distant station. 'Why have you come?' inquired the bishop. 'I want to be filled up; and the people tell me that I want to be filled up', was the man's reply.

How simple and true a confession: and how often, if we were quite sincere, we might make it of ourselves. No kind of work makes such demands as ministerial work. After much 'giving out' we become exhausted, and we are not alone in recognizing the fact. It is 'more life and fuller that we want'. How are we to get it?

To begin with, we must realize that we are entirely dependent upon the Divine supply to satisfy our need. We must come to the source of power, deeply conscious of our own unworthiness and insufficiency; 'poor in spirit', 'hungering and thirsting' to be 'filled'. That is the primary condition, the first necessity. It used to be maintained that 'nature abhors a vacuum.' Whether this be strictly true or not, we have good cause to believe that grace abhors a vacuum. The humble soul is not the soul which is sent empty away.

But our duty does not end when we have brought ourselves to feel our need of grace. There is a further necessity. We must prepare ourselves to seek it by diligent prayer. It is one thing to state the necessity in words, and another to give effect to it in practice. Indeed, this again is a matter which urgently calls for our serious attention.

We have already spoken of one grave defect in the religious life of our time. We shall have to refer to others. We do so because it is a safe rule that we should look within ourselves for the failings and shortcomings which are most readily seen without. We are intimately linked with the life around us. We share in its movements, and are influenced by the forces which tell upon its character. It is for this reason that we do wisely to study it even when our immediate purpose is the consideration of the needs of our own individual life.

Now on all sides to-day we have the complaint that there is little power of prayer. How constantly we are being told by one and another, 'We find it so hard to pray. We can spend time in visiting, in attending committees, in teaching, in managing institutions, with far more ease and satisfaction than we can spend it in prayer. Our prayers are so poor and distracted. When we have been on our knees only a few minutes it seems like an hour. We know that it ought not to be so, yet so it is and we do not seem able to help it.'

All of us must have had this said to us again and again. Few of us need to travel outside our own inner experience for the corroborative evidence that will convince us that such confessions are true.

But if this be so, it must mean that there is utterly a fault among us. It is not necessary to adduce a long series of instances to prove that the great spiritual leaders and workers of the past have invariably been distinguished by the importance which they have assigned to prayer; and this, again, in spite of the fact that they may have differed most widely in their other beliefs and opinions.

Luther wrote of himself in the busiest part of his life, 'I have so much to do that I cannot get on without three hours a day of praying.' Of Borromeo, the saintly Cardinal of Milan, and of our own Bishop Andrewes, it was said that they were in the habit of spending five hours each day in meditation and prayer.

We are made painfully conscious, when we read of experiences like these, that in spite of all our activities and studies we have need that some one should teach us afresh the very principles of religious life and work. There must be something radically wrong when modern reformers, and even modern divines, are perpetually announcing that it is only with the greatest difficulty that they can 'find time' for any prayers at all.

A more serious symptom could scarcely be. Prayer has been aptly described as 'the pulse of the soul.' Where prayer is strong and frequent, there the soul is in health and prospers; when prayer is intermittent and feeble, the life flags, moral duties begin to wear a forbidding aspect, and even the practical activities, which at first seemed able to take care of themselves, are found to lack the inward support without which they too, sooner or later, must inevitably fail.

If, then, we had need to seek out the causes for the lack of penitence, we have certainly no less need to seek out the causes for our want of prayer.

In looking for these, most of us will be inclined to turn first in a direction in which our thoughts have gone already. It is natural to suggest that a principal cause is to be discovered in the questionings that have arisen in consequence of the scientific teachings which have been specially characteristic of modern intellectual life; and here again it might be supposed that, in particular, the prominence given to the thought of 'law', in the sense of universal and unalterable sequence, must have led, in no small measure, to the paralysis which has made it so difficult for us to be in earnest about our prayers.

Without denying that there is truth in such a view, it is probably true also to say that a little while ago there would have been more reason to attach importance to this particular influence than there is at the present time. It is now far more generally recognized than it was, that law implies of necessity a lawgiver; and that 'government *by* law' is only an inaccurate expression for what is in reality government *according to* law. Moreover, the least consideration of what is perpetually taking place in our own experience suffices to show us, that the range within which we can avail ourselves of our knowledge of the working of laws, so as to produce effects which we desire, is a very wide one. It follows that it is manifestly impossible to set limits to the operations of a mind and will possessed of wisdom and power immeasurably superior to our own. For those by whom these fundamental axioms are intelligently grasped, the difficulties as to prayer, which arise from purely scientific considerations, become reduced—it is scarcely too bold to say—to quite inconsiderable proportions.[1]

On the whole, therefore, it is probable that we must seek the explanation we are in search of in another direction altogether; and it may well be that, when it is found, it will prove to be surprisingly simple.

We are essentially a practical people, and as such are strongly utilitarian. We are ready enough to make effort when we are certain that we shall be repaid for our pains. Now with many, perhaps with most of us, the question which we need to have answered in regard to prayer is this: Does it practically make much difference whether we pray or do not? If we were convinced that it did, we should have more heart to pray, and to persevere in prayer in spite of anything that might tempt us from it.

Our question in fact reduces itself to this: granted that the Divine Being is as free—and of course He must be—to comply with our requests as we are ourselves when asked to do some service for one another; can we be absolutely certain that He wishes us to pray, and that He has made the fulfilment of His purposes in any real sense to depend upon our prayers?

We may frankly admit that it is by no means obvious that this should be so. Even if we start from the conception of God as our Father, the conception which we feel to be the highest that we can form of Him, it by no means follows as of necessity that we should go to Him with the account of our needs and desires. An earthly parent might quite conceivably say to his children, 'Believe me, I am wiser than you are; I know what is best for you. I will do what is right. It is not in the least necessary that you should ask me for anything.'

[1] I would call attention to the following remarkable words: 'The supposition that there is any inconsistency between the acceptance of the constancy of natural order, and a belief in the efficacy of prayer, is the more unaccountable as it is obviously contradicted by analogies furnished by everyday experience. The belief in the efficacy of prayer depends upon the assumption that there is sombody, somewhere, who is strong enough to deal with the earth and its contents as men deal with the things and events which they are strong enough to modify or control; and who is capable of being moved by appeals such as men make to one another.'—Thomas Huxley, *Nineteenth Century,* Nov. 1887.

Without question, the Heavenly Father might have so ordered His dealings with us. He is infinitely above us. We are short-sighted and ignorant. He is wise and good. It might indeed seem reasonable that we should leave ourselves in His hands, and receive in silence what He saw best to send. We might even argue that it must be presumptuous on our part to suggest what His gifts are to be.

Quite possibly, if we had to be guided by our reasonings alone, we might arrive at the conclusion that this on the whole is the attitude most fitting for us to adopt. As we know, not a few persons have thought right to adopt it.

And yet, even if we could reason ourselves into taking this point of view, it is not likely that most of us could remain satisfied with it. Something within us would most assuredly rebel; a deep, strong instinct of the heart would rise in wrath to challenge the conclusion of the intellect. After all, we should feel that a true parent would be much more likely to use a different language. He would be much more likely to say, 'My children, I love you; I know all your needs; but I want to be far more than a provider. I want your confidence and your affection. I have want to have a very close relationship with you. I want you to tell me your thoughts and needs. Ask me for whatever you think would be good for you. If it is good, I will grant it; if not, I will give what is better.'

Who does not see at once that this would be a much more fatherly way? Which of us does not feel that a God whose pleasure it was to treat His children thus—'a God so nigh in all that we call upon Him for'—would be a God towards whom we could be much more readily drawn in reverence and in love?

But happily, as Christians, we are not left to be guided by either our reasonings or our feelings in so vitally important a matter. There is a Voice which speaks to us with final authority in regard to the great truths of the spiritual world. 'No man hath seen God at any time; the only begotten Son, which is in the bosom of the Father, He hath declared Him.' And no part of the revelation is more emphatically clear than the teaching as to the duty of prayer.

For an example we need go no further than the opening sermon in which are preserved for us those most elementary utter-
ances of our Lord's public ministry which have been happily
described as the 'commonplaces of Christ'. It is to the sixth
chapter of St Matthew's Gospel that we are accustomed to turn
for well-known statements as to the dependence of men upon
the care and the forethought of their Father in heaven. If He
provides for the birds and the flowers, much more will He pro-
vide for His children. He knows the things they have need of.
Such are the assurances which are to ennoble life, and banish
the anxieties which contract and degrade it.

Are we then to argue that no room is left for prayer? By no
means. Almost in the same breath, our Lord goes on to say,
'Ask and it shall be given you, seek and ye shall find, knock and
it shall be opened unto you; for every one that asketh receiveth,
and he that seeketh findeth, and to him that knocketh it shall
be opened.' And then, as if it were His intention to answer by
anticipation the questionings that were likely to arise, and to
render misgiving impossible, our Lord proceeds to apply the
conclusions which are most rightly to be drawn from the ana-
logy of the home: 'If ye then being evil know how to give good
gifts to your children, how much more shall your Father which
is in heaven give good things'—and let us notice especially the
emphasis laid upon the words which immediately follow—*'to
them that ask Him?'*

It is not our purpose to write a treatise on the Scriptural
doctrine of prayer, or we should make it our business to show
how this teaching of our Lord was foreshadowed in the writings
of the Old Testament, as for instance in 1 Kings 18:1, 42;
Ezek. 36:36, 37; Ps. 2:8, passages which will repay most atten-
tive consideration—and how completely it entered into the
thought and experience of His Apostles.

What it does concern us to make sure of here is the central
fact that it is the Divine will, as that will is expressed to us by
Him Who knew it as none other can know, that 'men ought
always to pray' (St Luke 18:1); that God requires our prayers,
and that it is His habit to grant us His gifts in response to them.

To express all this in the simplest monosyllables—*if we want we must ask.* That is the principle of prayer. 'Ask and ye shall have.' 'Ye have not because ye ask not.'

There is no hint in the teaching of our Lord that by our prayers we can change the Divine intentions. The perfect prayer will always find its fullest expression in the petition, 'Thy will be done' (see St Matt. 6:10, and 26:42). A wish to alter the will of the Father would be presumptuous indeed; would seem to be almost a blasphemy. Very different is the office of prayer as understood in the Christian sense.

Prayer is for us the appointed means whereby God has ordained to accomplish His purposes of blessing. When He determines to bless, He moves His servants to pray. The 'prayer of faith' is the prayer which is inspired by a certain conviction as to a definite intention on the part of God. 'This is the confidence that we have in Him, that if we ask anything according to His will He heareth us: and if we know that He hear us whatsoever we ask, we know that we have the petitions that we desired of Him.'[1]

Would it not make all the difference to our estimate of the value of prayer if we could grasp afresh this simple truth that God waits for our prayers, and makes it His rule to give in response to them? Let us think of some of the practical results that might be expected to follow from such a belief.

1. In the first place we should realize more than we have done that *prayer is work.* We have no difficulty in persuading ourselves that prayer is preparation for work. It is in very truth much more; *Orare est laborare*—to pray is to work. To pray is to put into operation a cause in order to produce an effect. 'The supplication of a righteous man availeth much in its working.' 'Prayer moves the Arm that moves the worlds, To bring salvation down.' Time is well spent that is spent on our knees in the study or in the church.

2. Those who pray much are increasingly convinced that *prayer is high work.* Havè we not been guilty of making a serious mistake in the way in which we have sometimes allowed ourselves to speak about prayer? How common it is to hear it suggested, 'If you cannot do anything else, at least you can

[1] 1 St John 5:14 f.

pray.' Surely that must be wrong. Surely it would be more true
to say, 'If you can pray, if you have in any degree acquired the
holy art, then for God's sake and man's sake do not do anything
else. Give yourself to it; continue on the mount with hands up-
raised. There will be no lack of fighters down below, who will
triumph by the help of your prayers.'

In order to realize the place in work which should be assigned
to prayer, we need but recall the thought of the consecutive
stages of the ministry of our Lord. At its beginning that ministry chiefly consisted of the active occupations of preaching, and
teaching, and healing. Then followed the passive stage of
suffering. That also was work, and higher work. Have we not
many a time found ourselves saying as we stood by the side of
the sufferer, 'My brother', or 'My sister, think not that you are
condemned to idleness, or set aside as useless, because you can
no longer go hither and thither and do the things that you did.
Believe it, you have been called to a more mysterious and more
far-reaching service. The best blessings that have come to our
race have come through pierced hands. We may not understand
it fully, but nevertheless it is true that our greatest benefactors
have been the sufferers. Rejoice that to you also has been granted some share of their privilege.'

But His ministry did not end with suffering. After He had
suffered He rose and went on high. He had said, 'It is expedient
for you that I go.' 'I go unto My Father . . . and I will pray.'
Now 'He ever liveth to make intercession for us.' 'Thou art our
Moses out of sight: Speak for us or we perish quite.' Must we
not believe that this, the mediatorial ministry, is a stage yet
higher than either of the preceding?

Time was when the Church saw it to be her wisdom to call
aside those of her children who had clearly a vocation for
prayer, in order that they might devote the chief energies of
their lives to the holy task of intercession. Such a time may
come again.[1] In the meanwhile we must do all we can to make it
clear that we know of no work that ranks higher than the work
of prayer.

3. Those who have rightly grasped the importance of prayer

[1] It has—Ed.

will not marvel greatly if they find by experience that *prayer is hard work*. All high work is hard work.

No man has possessed the faculty for abstract thinking in a greater degree than did Samuel Taylor Coleridge; yet it was Coleridge who declared that, 'Of all mental exercises earnest prayer is the most severe.' It is not difficult to see why it must be so. For earnest prayer, all the higher powers must needs be employed—reasoning, imagination, affection, conscience, and will—and further, all must be bent and united in a single aim.

It is no easy thing to 'gird up' the powers of mind and spirit. We have often noticed how difficult a person whose days are spent in manual labour finds the performance of some simple task which happens to require the use of his brain. Perspiration will start to the brow of a labourer as he awkwardly handles the pen and attempts to enter his name in the vestry register. Half a day's work in the fields would have taken less out of him! And there are multitudes who have not any more power of using their souls. A very few minutes spent in a serious effort of prayer leave them completely exhausted.

Nor is the feeling of strain confined to beginners. Even those who by continual use have had their spiritual senses exercised have known what it was to be brought by their pleading in prayer to the verge of an utter prostration. Like Jacob of old, who 'had power with God and prevailed', they have carried for long the marks of the conflict.

Nay further, we may even appeal to the experience of Him who is greater than the greatest of His saints.

If we would really know what the labour of prayer may involve, we must go to the Garden and see Him under the olives bowed down to the earth. There as He 'prayed', and 'prayed again more earnestly', so great was His agony that—we note it with reverence and wonder—'His sweat was as it were great drops of blood falling down to the ground.'

4. Once more, with no hesitation let us say it, *prayer is our work*. 'We will give ourselves continually to prayer, and to the ministry of the word'—and in that order—was the determination of the Apostles. 'Let him call for the elders of the church, and let them pray', was the direction of St James. He

can have little of the true spirit of a Christian who has no longing to bear some part in that ministry of intercession in which
he knows that his great High Priest is ceaselessly engaged.

But if prayer is to be with us a work, it will have to be
regulated by method. It has been truly insisted that 'no one will
make much of prayer who does not make a business of it.' We
may not wait for times of special emotion, ready as we must
be to use them when they come. There must be a definite rule.
We must win ourselves to our high task by varying the details
of it. Subjects must be assigned to the different days: lists of
intercession must be kept, and answers must be noted as they
are received. A book systematically used for this purpose becomes in the course of years a most unassailable witness to the
efficacy of persevering prayer.

Would indeed that we might realize that this is the work to
which we have been specially called, and of which it is not too
much to say that God is ever waiting to accept it at our hands.
There are those who may be qualified to undertake many parts
of the work of a parish; but who will make good the losses that
are incurred by an unprayerful priest? On the other hand, who
can measure the gains, in all departments of work, where the
pastor is known and felt to be a man of prayer?

'Whilst we may find instances of success, and sometimes of
great and unlikely success,' said Bishop Wilberforce, 'in the
ministry of those who have lacked almost every other qualification, there can, I believe, be no instances found of a successful ministry which was not full of prayers.'[1]

It would be possible to tell of one of our number who for
years has made intercession the central reality of his life and
work. He is the vicar in a village of which the church stands
apart on the summit of a considerable hill. When the nights are
dark and the wind is rising, it has long been his practice to go
up to the church and kindle the beacon on the tower as a
guide to the fisher-folk away in the offing. They see the light,
as it flashes over the waters, and they know that the good priest
who sustains it is spending the intervals of the night in the
church in prayer for their souls and their bodies. It is little mar-

[1] *Addresses to Candidates for Ordination,* p. 144.

vel that there is almost nothing they will not do for him in return.

Let us be the best students, and preachers, and organizers we may; but above all, and before all, let us covet to pray. So only shall we ourselves be filled with the Holy Ghost, and be made centres of spiritual influence. Happy indeed are the parishes where the priests, and the people after them, have learned to pray!

Note

The following passage from William Law's *Serious Call* (chap. 21.) illustrates remarkably the effects of a habit of prayer upon both the worker and the work:

Ouranius is a holy priest, full of the spirit of the Gospel, watching, labouring, and praying for a poor country village. Every soul in it is as dear to him as himself; and he loves them all, as he loves himself; because he prays for them all, as often as he prays for himself.

If his whole life is one continual exercise of great zeal and labour, hardly ever satisfy'd with any degrees of care and watchfulness, 'tis because he has learn'd the great value of souls, by so often appearing before God, as an intercessor for them.

He never thinks he can love, or do enough for his flock; because he never considers them in any other view, than as so many persons, that by receiving the gifts and graces of God, are to become his hope, his joy, and his crown of rejoicing.

He goes about his Parish, and visits everybody in it, but he visits in the same spirit of piety that he preaches to them; he visits them to encourage their virtues, to assist them with his advice and counsel, to discover their manner of life, and to know the state of their souls, that he may intercede with God for them according to their particular necessities.

When Ouranius first entered into holy orders, he had a haughtiness in his temper, a great contempt and disregard for all foolish and unreasonable people; but he has pray'd away this spirit, and has now the greatest tenderness for the most obstinate sinners; because he is always hoping, that God will sooner or later hear those prayers that he makes for their repentance.

The rudeness, ill-nature, or perverse behaviour of any flock, used at first to betray him into impatience; but it now raises no other passion in him, than a desire of being upon his knees in prayer to God for them. Thus have his prayers for others alter'd and amended the state of his own heart.

It would strangely delight you to see with what spirit he converses, with what tenderness he reproves, with what affection he exhorts, and with what vigor he preaches; and 'tis all owing to this, because he reproves, exhorts, and preaches to those for whom he first prays to God.

This devotion softens his heart, enlightens his mind, sweetens his temper, and makes everything that comes from him, instructive, amiable, and affecting.

At his first coming to his little village, it was as disagreeable to him as a prison, and every day seem'd too tedious to be endured in so retir'd a place. He thought his parish was too full of poor and mean people, that were none of them fit for the conversation of a Gentleman.

This put him upon a close application to his studies. He kept much at home, writ notes upon Homer and Plautus, and sometimes thought it hard to be called to pray by any poor body, when he was just in the midst of one of Homer's battels.

This was his polite, or I may rather say, poor, ignorant turn of mind, before devotion had got the government of his heart.

But now his days are so far from being tedious, or his Parish too great a retirement, that he now only wants more time to do that variety of good which his soul thirsts after. The solitude of his little parish is become matter of great comfort to him, because he hopes that God' has plac'd him and his flock there, to make it their way to heaven.

He can now not only converse with, but gladly attend and wait upon the poorest kind of people. He is now daily watching over the weak and infirm, humbling himself to perverse, rude, ignorant people, wherever he can find them; and is so far from desiring to be considered as a Gentleman, that he desires to be used as the servant of all; and in the spirit of his Lord and Master girds himself, and is glad to kneel down and wash any of their feet.

He now thinks the poorest creature in his Parish good enough, and great enough, to deserve the humblest attendances, the kindest friendships, the tenderest offices, he can possibly shew them.

He is so far now from wanting agreeable company, that he thinks there is no better conversation in the world, than to be talking with poor and mean people about the kingdom of heaven.

All these noble thoughts and divine sentiments are the effects of his great devotion; he presents every one so often before God in his prayers, that he never thinks he can esteem, reverence, or serve those enough, for whom he implores so many mercies from God.

Ouranius is mightily affected with this passage of holy Scripture: *The effectual fervent prayer of a righteous man availeth much.*

This makes him practise all the arts of holy living, and aspire after every instance of piety and righteousness, that his prayers for his flock may have their full force, and avail much with God.

For this reason he has sold a small estate that he had, and has erected a charitable retirement for ancient, poor people to live in prayer and piety, that his prayers being assisted by such good works, may pierce the clouds, and bring down blessings upon these souls committed to his care.

Ouranius reads how God himself said unto Abimelech concerning Abraham, *He is a prophet; he shall pray for thee, and thou shalt live.* And again, how he said of Job, *And my servant Job shall pray for you; for him will I accept.*

From these passages Ouranius justly concludes, that the prayers of men eminent for holiness of life, have an extraordinary power with God; that He grants to other people such pardons, reliefs and blessings, through their prayers, as would not be granted to men of less piety and perfection. This makes Ouranius exceeding studious of christian perfection, searching after every grace and holy temper, purifying his heart all manner of ways, fearful of every error and defect in his life, lest his prayers for his flock should be less availing with God, through his own defects in holiness.

This makes him careful of every temper of his heart, give alms of all that he hath, watch, and fast, and mortify, and live according to the strictest rules of temperance, meekness, and humility, that he may be in some degree like an Abraham, or a Job in his Parish, and make such prayers for them as God will hear and accept.

These are the happy effects, which a devout intercession hath produc'd in the life of Ouranius.

Chapter 5

Devotion to Our Lord

We have endeavoured to indicate some of the directions in which effort is most likely to be valuable in enabling us to gain more fully for ourselves the power of Divine grace, and to become the instruments whereby that power may be brought to bear afresh upon the hearts and consciences of others. We have named penitence and prayer as two conditions, indispensable at all times, upon which it would seem to be necessary to lay particular emphasis at the present time.

We must go further yet. Much as we should rightly insist upon the need of both penitence and prayer, we may not suppose that they represent all that is to be required of those who are to attain to a full growth of Christian experience. Indeed we have only to reflect for a moment to feel that this is so. In themselves neither penitence nor prayer are distinctly and exclusively Christian. All other religions have in some degree made them a part of their discipline. At the most they represent the preparation of the soil in which the higher life is to develop, and the welcoming of the influences which promote that development, rather than the completed perfection of flower and the fruit. For this another condition must needs be fulfilled.

On the closing page of the Gospels there is contained what we might not inaptly describe as an examination paper intended to test proficiency in discipleship. It consists of but three questions, and they are all alike: 'Lovest thou Me?' Christianity can only have its perfect work in us as we set ourselves to learn the lesson of absolute devotion to our Lord.

However often we may have pondered the matter, and however familiar the thought of it may be to us, we cannot do otherwise than give it its place when we are dealing with the requirements of personal life. And again we shall make it our aim to be as simple and practical as possible.

To begin with, then, let us ask, In what does devotion consist?

Devotion—the noblest fact in human story—may be of two kinds. There is, in the first place, devotion to a *cause*; as, for example, to the cause of knowledge, or justice, or social reform. Men have given themselves, times without number, to serve the interests of these; and very splendid and uplifting their devotion has been.

And there is a yet loftier devotion than this. It is devotion to a *person*: the loyalty of a pupil to his master, or a soldier to his leader; the affection of parent and child, of husband and wife, of brother, or sister, or friend—an even more enkindling and powerful devotion.

Someone has exquisitely said that, 'To love is the perfect of the verb to live.' Devotion is love when it has found the object which can draw from it the very best that it has to give.

When we ask which of these devotions it is that our Lord requires from His followers, we have to answer unhesitatingly that He requires them both. He calls upon us to consecrate all that we have unreservedly to His cause, bidding us count ourselves happy if we may suffer for it. But, first and foremost, He asks for devotion to His Person. It is 'For My sake, and the Gospel's'. We must many times have felt it to be in the highest degree remarkable that He, who more than all besides was 'meek and lowly in heart', should so often and so earnestly insist that His Person is to be the object of supremest affection. 'He that loveth father or mother more than Me is not worthy of Me.' 'If any man come to Me, and hate not his father, and mother, and wife, and children, and brethren, and sisters, yea, and his own life also, he cannot be My disciple.' No language which He could have used could have spoken more strongly than that.

And there can be no question that, all through the ages, He has obtained what He has asked. High as is the demand, the response has not proved to be impossible. From its earliest days the passion for Christ's Person has been the unfailing character-

istic of a living Christianity. The beautiful legend that the heart
of Ignatius, when recovered after his martyrdom, was found
to be inscribed with the name of Christ, is true to the spirit
of the faith as it has existed from the first. It was the love of
their Master that inspired generation after generation of con-
fessors to bear their witness in defiance of threatenings and
tortures. The flame of devotion burned with an ardour which
no power on earth was able to quench. The world, which was
not in the secret, when it witnessed the joy and tested to the
utmost the endurance of the Christians, could only conclude
that they must be possessed by some quite unintelligible
madness.

Would that some one might write down for us a history of
the exploits which from those days to our own have had their
origin in devotion to the Person of our Lord! When it is written,
it may well carry on its forefront the remarkable words, familiar to most of us, which are said to have been uttered in his
exile by Napoleon I.

'Jesus Christ was more than man . . . . I have inspired multitudes with such an enthusiastic devotion that they would have
died for me, . . . but to do this it was necessary that I should
be visibly present with the electric influence of my looks, of
my words, of my voice. When I saw men and spoke to them, I
lighted up the flame of self-devotion in their hearts. . . . Christ
alone has succeeded in so raising the mind of man toward the
Unseen, that it becomes insensible to the barriers of time and
space. Across a chasm of eighteen hundred years, Jesus Christ
makes a demand which is beyond all others difficult to satisfy;
He asks for that which a philosopher may often seek in vain at
the hands of his friends, or a father of his children, or a bride
of her spouse, or a man of his brother. He asks for the human
heart; He will have it entirely to Himself. He demands it uncon-
ditionally; and forthwith His demand is granted. Wonderful!
In defiance of time and space, the soul of man, with all its
powers and faculties, becomes an annexation to the empire of
Christ. All who sincerely believe in Him experience that supernatural love towards Him. This phenomenon is unaccountable:
it is altogether beyond the scope of man's creative powers.'[1]

[1] The above is the translation given by Dr Liddon in *The Divinity of Christ*. For
evidence of the historical accuracy of the reported conversation, see the long note on
pages 150 and 151 of that work.

Let us be certain, then, that Christians are Christ's men—disciples, soldiers, freedmen, of their Lord. And let us be certain also that, if the power of Christianity is to be renewed at any time, it can only be by the renewal of this holy attachment to the Person of Christ. Zeal for doctrines, adherence to system, these sooner or later will slacken and give way. Only one motive can be relied on to keep us at our task, amid discouragements and disappointments, and when the heats of youth are over. One power alone will suffice to expel selfishness, to curb impatience, to inspire gentleness, and to banish timidity.

Our practical question, therefore, is this: How can devotion to our Lord be quickened and strengthened in our hearts? By what that we can do should we strive to increase it? Emotions are hard to excite, and still harder to maintain; indeed, as we know, they are not by any means always subject to our control. How then can we hope to be able to make this highest passion the master force in our lives?

The answer may be given in two parts:

1. Love to our Lord is, as a rule, the outcome of a consciousness of His love to us. The highest devotion has ever been the fruit of 'the faith of the Son of God who loved me, and gave Himself for me'.

Political economists tell us of a 'magic of property'. By this is meant the quite new interest which a man is wont to feel in a thing when he can say of it that it is his very own; an interest which inclines him to make efforts, and even sacrifices he would never otherwise have dreamt of making. This 'magic of property' has something corresponding to it in spiritual experience. It is when the truth is brought home to us that we have a strictly personal interest and share in the great facts of the Divine redemption, that we are able to appropriate their value and force in such a degree as to make them the joy and inspiration of our lives.

May we not rightly say that it is one purpose of the Sacraments thus to bring home to our hearts and minds our personal interest in 'our common salvation'? Who but has felt the soul-stirring power of the words, 'The Body of our Lord Jesus Christ, which was given *for thee*'?

The great moments of life are those in which—at the altar, in some quiet spot of nature, over a book, or through the experience of an earthly friendship—there has been granted a new hint or assurance of the 'love of Christ which passeth knowledge'. It has been the story of that love which has arrested the attention and agitated the heart of many a lad and girl in the freshness of early youth; yes, and of many an earnest priest and vigorous layman, filling them with the longing to do something for Him who counted no surrender too great to make for them.

2.   But if the love to our Lord, which has been awakened by the thought of all that He has done for us, is to continue as a permanent force in our lives, it must needs be strengthened and sustained by devout meditation upon what He was, and therefore is, in Himself. It is while we are thus 'musing' that 'the fire burns'. From the first feelings of gratitude and admiration the true disciples pass little by little to the self-forgetful adoration of perfected devotion.

Do we realize as we should how remarkable is the provision that has been made for our growth in the knowledge of Christ? The more we think of it, the more we are impressed by its variety and completeness. With no fear of contradiction we may assert that, in the whole compass of recorded history, there exists no such wealth of materials for the knowledge of any individual as can compare with that which we have in the Gospels for the knowledge of our Lord. In those wonderful biographies we have pictures of what He was, taken from four very different points of view. In one we are allowed to see clearly what in another is left in shade. We can combine them as we do the pictures in the stereoscope. As we continue to gaze, the natural surroundings, the historical conditions, the lake, the Judaean hills, the Mount of Olives, the keenly marked Jewish faces, stand out graphically before us; and, above all, the minutest details of the principal figure, His deeds, His words, His very looks, become extraordinarily vivid and real.

So perfectly is this the case that the words of Erasmus, bold as they may appear, contain no exaggeration. That scholarly student did not scruple to say, 'These writings bring back to you the living image of that most holy mind, the very Christ Himself speaking, healing, dying, rising, in fact so entirely present, that you would see less of Him if you beheld Him with your eyes.'[1]

And long before the days of Erasmus thoughtful men had learned to understand how inexhaustible are the resources of knowledge which are available to us in the Gospel presentations of our Lord. They saw with loving delight that there is no relationship, no set of social conditions, no problem of suffering, no one of the numberless circumstances of the most ordinary life, which does not receive its illumination from Him who is the Light of the world.

How delightfully ardent and simple, for instance, are the following words in which one such spoke of the details to be noted by those who would make full use of the sacred narrative. Our feeling as we read his list is that he might have gone on with it for ever!

Always and everywhere have Him devoutly before the eyes of your mind, in His behaviour and in His ways; as when He is with His disciples and when He is with sinners; when He speaks and when He preaches; when He goes forth and when He sits down; when He sleeps and when He wakes; when He eats and when He serves others; when He heals the sick, and when He does His other miracles; setting forth to thyself in thy heart His ways and His doings, how humbly He bore Himself among men, how tenderly among His disciples, how pitiful He was to the poor, to whom He made Himself like in all things, and who seemed to be His own special family; how He despised none nor shrunk from them, not even from the leper; how He paid no court to the rich, how free He was from the cares of the world, and from trouble about the needs of the body; how patient under insult, and how gentle in answering, for He sought not to maintain His cause by keen and bitter words, but with gentle and humble answer to cure another's malice; what composure in all His behaviour, what anxiety for the salvation of souls, for the love of whom He also deigned to die; how He offered Himself as the pattern of all that is good; how compassionate He was to the afflicted, how He condescended to the imperfection of the weak, how He despised not sinners; how mercifully He received the penitent, how dutiful He was to His parents, how ready in serving all, according to His own words, 'I am among you as he that doth serve'; how He shunned all display and show of singularity; how He avoided all occasions of offence; how temperate in eating and drinking, how modest in appearance, how earnest in prayer, how sober in His

---

[1] The original of the passage is prefixed to the Greek Testament edited by Westcott and Hort.

watching, how patient of toil and want; how peaceful and calm in all things.[1]

We live in the age of books. They pour out upon us from the press in an ever-increasing multitude. And we are always reading. Manuals, text-books, articles, books of devotion, books of criticism, books about the Bible, books about the Gospels, are devoured with avidity. But what amount of time and labour do we give to the consideration of the Gospels themselves?

We are constantly tempted to imagine that we 'get good' more quickly by reading some modern statement of truth, which we find is comparatively easy to appropriate because it is presented to us in a shape and from a standpoint with which our education, or it may be party association, has made us familiar. But the good that we acquire readily is not that which enters most deeply into our being, and becomes an abiding possession.

It would be well if we could realize quite simply that nothing worth the having is to be gained without the winning. The great truths of nature are not offered to us in such a form as makes it easy to grasp them: the treasures of grace must be sought with all the skill and energy which are characteristic of the man who is searching for goodly pearls.

The patient, intelligent study of the fourfold Gospel is a task not of weeks but of years. But here again, as in the case of prayer, we should be encouraged to persevere if only we could be certain that the effort expended would secure a return such as can be obtained by no other means. And may we not be certain?

It is no uncommon thing to hear complaints about the want of force in religious people to-day. 'We have goodness,' said an acute observer who lately passed from among us, 'but we lack character.' Amid much that is excellent there is little that makes an impression. Can it be doubted that one chief reason for this is to be traced in the too general failure to go direct to the original sources of our knowledge of the Person of our Lord?

[1] Ludolfus de Saxonia (1330). *Proœm. in Vitam Christi*; quoted by Dean Church, *Human Life and its Conditions*, pp. 192 f.

Sometimes, as we know, an illustration will at once convey to the mind a more rapid and exact description of that which we wish to make plain than could be conveyed by the most cogent of logical statements. Let us try what such help can do for us in the present case.[1]

You are a visitor, let us suppose, in Florence, and have found your way into the studio of an artist there. Your attention is immediately arrested by a painting of a masterpiece which you have seen in one or the other of the world-famous galleries. You venture a question as to the price it might be expected to fetch. The amount named is so large as to be virtually prohibitory. In a moment or two, however, another painting is produced which for aught you are able to see exactly resembles the first. This you are told you may have at a much more moderate figure. The difference is so marked that you express your astonishment, and ask an explanation. The reason given is this. That first copy was made in the gallery. In order to obtain the necessary permission, the painter had to put down his name on a list and to wait, it may have been several years, until his turn arrived. At last he had found himself in the presence of the Raphael, or the Titian, or the Correggio, whichever it may have been. There you could have seen him seated with his easel and canvas. But days passed by before he began his work. Intently he pored over each line, and each tone of colour. After a while the face began to grow upon him, until the vision of it passed down with him into the street, followed him to his home, and haunted his imagination as he lay on his bed at night. Then he took up his brush, and it seemed as if the spirit of the old master had possessed him, and were directing his hand. The picture completed, he carried it off with pride. Many have been the reproductions that he has made from it since. One of these you may have, as he tells you; but the first he will not part with if he can help it. He knows, if you do not, that there is all the difference in the world between a copy of a copy, and the copy of the original.

And is not this just the difference that we so often feel, and

[1] The illustration which follows was suggested to me many years ago by a nonconformist minister, whose name I cannot remember, as we were travelling together on the continent. I have never ceased to be grateful to him for it.

find so difficult to account for? We meet with persons who have seriously resolved to set before themselves a standard of spiritual attainment. What they have done is this. They have fixed upon an individual whom they admire, whom they have seen, or of whom they have read in a book; and they have determined to be 'like that'. The result is what we see. There is much that is praiseworthy, little perhaps with which it would be easy to find any particular fault; and yet we are conscious that something is wanting—indeed we might almost go so far as to say everything is wanting—which gives its distinction and interest to character. Yes! this is what is wrong; at the most they are copies of copies.

Then it happens, once and again, alas! all too rarely, that we meet with a different experience. We are privileged to know some one who has said, 'I will go straight to the Gospels. I will set my gaze upon Him who alone is full of grace and truth. In Him only shall I behold the ideal of beauty. In His fulness alone can I hope to discover what my own particular life was intended to be. Let me know more and more what He was like. Let me be filled with His Spirit; if so be that I may, in ever so small a degree, show forth any of the lineaments of His perfect manhood.' And again we have seen the result. There has been a freshness, a fearlessness, a freedom from conventionality, combined with a humility, a reverence, a patience, which have unmistakably betokened a character that has derived its impress and drawn its inspiration from the highest possible source. In short, what we have seen is a copy of the Original.

Happy would it be if we could count that day a lost day which has not added something to our understanding of that Original. When shall we believe that there is no honour which earth has in its power to bestow, that is for a moment to be compared with the honour we receive when those to whom we minister are constrained to take knowledge that there is anything in our lives which in any way reminds them of their Lord?

Note I

A striking example of what the imitation of Christ can mean under modern conditions is to be found in the remarkable passage in which his biographer describes what the Person of Christ had become to F. W. Robertson of Brighton. Those who remember it will be thankful to see it again.

The Incarnation was to him the centre of all History, the blossoming of Humanity. The Life which followed the Incarnation was the explanation of the life of God, and the only solution of the life of man. He did not speak much of loving Christ: his love was fitly mingled with that veneration which makes love perfect; his voice was solemn, and he paused before he spoke His Name in common talk; for what that Name meant had become the central thought of his intellect, and the deepest realization of his spirit. He had spent a world of study, of reverent meditation, of adoring contemplation on the gospel history.

Nothing comes forward more visibly in his letters than the way in which he had entered into the human life of Christ. To that everything is referred—by that everything is explained. The gossip of a drawing-room, the tendencies of the time, the religious questions of the day, . . . the loneliness and the difficulties of his work, were not so much argued upon or combated, as at once and instinctively brought to the test of a Life which was lived out eighteen centuries ago, but which went everywhere with him.

Out of this intuitive reception of Christ, and from this ceaseless silence of meditation which makes the blessedness of great love, there grew up in him a deep comprehension of the whole, as well as a minute sympathy with all the delicate details of the character of Christ. Day by day, with passionate imitation, he followed his Master, musing on every action, revolving in thought the interdependence of all that Christ had said or done, weaving into the fibres of his heart the principles of the Life he worshipped, till he had received into his being the very impression and image of that unique Personality. His very doctrines were the Life of Christ expressed in words. The Incarnation, Atonement, and Resurrection of Christ were not dogmas to him. In himself he was daily realizing them. They were in him a life, a power, a light. This was his Christian consciousness.—*Life and Letters,* pp. 416 f.

Note II

The following extract from a sermon preached by the Rev. Charles Marriott was included by Bishop King in an address to the members of the Lambeth Conference of 1898 at their Devotional Day:

What is reason, but a partaking of the Light that lighteth every man that cometh into the world? what is poetry, but the burning of the heart when He is near? what is art, but the striving to recollect His lineaments? what is history, but the traces of His iron rod or His Shepherd's staff?

Meditation on Him, prayer to Him, learning of Him, conformity to Him, partaking of Him, are the chief business of the Christian life.

To this last the Bishop added:

'Oh! if we had only made it so, how much happier, how much stronger, we might have been; how much stronger to help others, and to make them happy!'

Chapter 6

Secularization

It would be possible, no doubt, to name other directions in which we have need to direct our efforts if we are to succeed in upraising our level of personal life; but for our immediate purpose what has been said may be sufficient. Experience as teachers of others must have shown us that far more is gained as a rule by concentrating attention upon a few plain duties, than by setting out comprehensive schemes, which by their balanced completeness may satisfy the mind, but which through lack of definiteness fail to appeal to the conscience and influence the will. Penitence, and prayer, and the meditation which has for its object the increase of devotion to our Lord—these must produce far-reaching effects upon our life and upon our ministry.

But while it might not be wise to add to the list of duties, it may be of value that we should direct our thoughts to some of the dangers which specially beset the spiritual life of Christians to-day. It is, of course, true that no mere avoidance of dangers can ever be enough to keep us in the way of highest attainment; yet a clear recognition of the perils that surround us is of real use in helping us to walk more warily and resolutely in it.

It is not an easy thing to single out such dangers as we should agree to consider the most serious and widespread at the present time. The attempt must be made therefore with some hesitation. Here again it may be sufficient to mention but three.

The first place shall be given to the danger of *secularization;* to the temptation, that is to say, which would lead us to devote ourselves to a variety of pursuits other than those which properly belong to us, to such an extent as to obscure our character and weaken our influence as spiritual leaders.

Next we shall do well to think of the danger of *over-occupation;* and under that head we shall include the risks which we incur when we persist in the attempt to do too many things even of the kind that may be rightly included in our proper sphere.

And, lastly, something must be said of *depression,* the disposition to despair of ourselves and of others, which is often the penalty of a disregard of these earlier dangers, but which may also threaten the peace and well-being of those who have been the most successful in avoiding them.

First, then, the danger of *secularization.*

As we take note of what is going on around us, we cannot fail to be struck by the fact of a remarkable widening of the ordinary conceptions of public and individual duty. Never before has there been throughout society as a whole a keener or more sympathetic sense of the obligations which bind class to class, and man to man. Never has there been a time when more hearts more readily responded to the appeals which are made by misery and wrong; or when more hands were eager to 'do something' to improve the conditions and prospects of those who seem to be carrying an unequal share of the burdens of hardship and suffering.

In the movement to alleviate and remedy the evils of ignorance and pauperism and disease, the Church has been anxious to take an active and a leading part. Reading the problems of the age in the light of her inherited beliefs, she has been led to the most comprehensive views of the meaning of those beliefs, and of the whole purpose and scope of Christianity. Her message has been increasingly applied to phases and departments of human life and activity which had not been generally thought of as included in its range. The desire has grown stronger and stronger to prove that all interests, all occupations, all recreations, so far as they were not actually wrong in themselves, were to be regarded as entitled to a place in the programme of the Church.

With this broadening of the conception of the mission of the Church, there has come of necessity a widening of the sphere of work in which the clergy are expected to engage. The large culture, which is so valuable a part of their training, has made it possible for them to take their places freely and naturally in social efforts beside their fellows of the laity; the democratic tendency, which is everywhere felt, has given a further impulse to their inclination to enter sympathetically into all that in any way contributes to the life of the people: and, yet more, the earnest desire to win those who have seemed to be least accessible to the influences of religion has prompted them to devote time and energy to the study of their problems, as well as to schemes for their comfort and even for their amusement.

In any widening of understanding and sympathy we may heartily rejoice. It must be for good that the Gospel of the Incarnation is felt to be in the largest sense the Gospel of Life. It can only be matter for thankfulness whenever the clergy are foremost in urging the responsibilities which should weigh more heavily than they do upon all who have wealth and position: nor can they be too eager in welcoming efforts on behalf of those who are the least able to take care of themselves.

It by no means follows however that, amid these causes for thankfulness, there may not be reasons for anxiety, and even for alarm. In our mixed life the evil stands ever at the side of the good: and we have continually to be on our guard against the 'defects of our qualities', even when these are at their best. In this case what is to be feared is that the widening of which we have spoken is being gained at a very serious cost.

An artist and a clergyman were sitting together at dinner not long ago in London. In the course of their conversation the artist said: 'Ours is a philanthropic[1] age; ours is not a religious age.' Generalizations are confessedly dangerous, and we might well demur to so sweeping a statement. No one of us would have let it pass altogether unchallenged; and yet there is probably not one of us but would feel compelled to admit that a measure of truth underlies it. And certainly a statement of this kind, coming from a thoughtful layman, is calculated to make us pause and consider whether there is not a real peril before us all in the direction in which things are moving so easily.

The fear is lest, with the enlarging of the meaning of duty in one direction, there has been also a narrowing and lessening of its meaning in another, and that the very highest direction.

---

[1] Perhaps in the twentieth century we would use the term 'social service' here—Editor.

The word 'duty' is on all lips. We are proud of our pride in it. But what do we commonly mean by it? Is not the duty intended almost invariably that which a man owes to his fellow creatures; or possibly sometimes that which he owes to himself? How rarely is it the duty which he owes to his God! Even when all possible allowance has been made for the almost impenetrable reserve that characterizes an Englishman in regard to matters in which his intimate motives and feelings are involved, there are signs enough of a tendency which, if unchecked and uncorrected, can only lead to a gradual secularization of aims and ideals.

Unless the wisest of our teachers have been deceived, and unless the deepest lessons of history are to be distrusted, the end of social service itself will not be far distant when once social service is allowed to usurp the place which belongs to religion.

If the danger is real for others, we may be sure that it is real for us. We have already spoken of reasons which make it natural that the clergy should be inclined to throw themselves sympathetically into the social service movements of the time: we might easily add to them. Many are glad to welcome our assistance and leadership. There is the feeling that such activity helps to make the Church popular. We are anxious, it may be, to rebut a charge of narrowness. We feel that there is a gain in whatever brings us into living touch with the actual facts of ordinary experience. We see so perpetually the evils that are crying out for redress: and we have reason to know that we have gifts and qualifications which would enable us to deal effectively with them.

The fact that we may thus easily be drawn into the current which is setting so strongly about us, makes it the more necessary to speak plainly of the effects which have followed, and are not unlikely still to follow, in the life and ministry of those who with excellent intentions yield themselves unreservedly to the prevailing tendency.

No one would think of denying that there are, as there have been in the past, remarkable examples to prove that it is possible for men endowed with exceptional vitality to throw themselves into activities of the most varied kinds, and at the same time preserve their sense of proportion and with it the distinctive tone and character of the sacred office to which they were ordained. But then these are exceptional men. It is only too evident that, for the average man amongst us, such an attempt is more likely than not to lead to serious failure.

Instances have occurred in which it is scarcely too much to say that the priest and pastor has been merged and lost in the social leader and political reformer; or, more disastrous yet, in which he has descended to a level at which he has been regarded as little more than a successful provider of popular amusements. Even where things have stopped far short of this—and we freely admit that the extreme cases are rare—it has frequently happened that, in his anxiety to be forward in promoting schemes of practical benevolence, a clergyman has allowed himself to become immersed in affairs of the nature of the 'serving of tables', to the consequent neglect of the directly spiritual parts of his pastoral work.

Nowhere can the process of secularization be more clearly traced than in the preaching delivered from our pulpits. The old-fashioned doctrinal and expository discourse might not be well suited to the needs or capacities of a modern audience, but it might be instructive for many of us if it were possible to have the judgment of some of our predecessors upon the hurried, disjointed, up-to-date deliverances which too often do duty for sermons to-day.

The adopting of lay costume, and the abandonment of a certain gravity of demeanour, may seem small things in themselves; but they are not small things if they mean that, as the result of our desire to be 'all things to all men', we have made it not more easy but more difficult for them to turn to us in the hour when they become conscious of their need of the higher aid which it is our mission to bring them.

The truth is that we have need constantly to go back to the first principles of our ministerial vocation, and to renew our sense of its purpose and aim. We should be greatly helped to do this were we to make it a practice to read carefully from time to time the service which was used at our ordination as priests. How plainly it set forth to us the expectations we were to form of the life-work opening before us. How good it is for us to compare those expectations with our actual experience!

Notice the three words on which marked emphasis is laid in the Exhortation addressed by the Bishop to the candidates. 'Dignity', 'Difficulty', 'Duty': these may fitly sound as watch-words in our ears. We dare not lower our conception of our responsibility as 'Messengers, Watchmen, and Stewards of the Lord'. It is necessary that we should often be reminded that it can be no light task to 'compass the doing of so weighty a work, pertaining to the salvation of man'; and that we may only hope to accomplish it as we 'apply ourselves wholly to this one thing, and draw all our cares and studies this way'. The serious pondering of the Ordinal, with its solemn injunctions and no less solemn promises, would do much to 'print in our remembrance' that our main concern after all is not the re-arranging of the social order, however powerfully we may con-tribute indirectly to this by our labour for the Church of God, and by our endeavours to 'set forwards quietness, peace, and love among all Christian people'.

The Ordinal tells us that if we are to 'wax riper and stronger' in our ministry, it must be 'by daily reading and weighing of the Scriptures'. We have already considered the necessity for a con-tinued study of the Gospels. We may add to what has been said that there are special reasons why, at this particular time, we should try to get a just view of the attitude which our Lord assumed towards social questions. The idea has become widely prevalent that this attitude was very much more that of the modern reformer than has ordinarily been recognized by the Church in the past; and all of us know how readily an idea that is popularly accepted may possess the minds even of thoughtful students in a degree greatly in excess of the measure of truth which it represents. That in this case the popular view may be seriously challenged, and that a reaction from it is not unlikely to set in before long, may perhaps be gathered from such utter-ances as the following, coming to us as they do from very dif-ferent quarters.

In a valuable work, *Jesus Christ and the Social Question,* pp. 78 f., Professor Peabody of Harvard writes:

There was political oppression about Him to be remedied, there were social unrighteousness and iniquity to be condemned; but Jesus does not fling Himself into these social issues of His time. He moves through them with a strange tranquillity, not as one who is indifferent to them, but as one whose eye is fixed on an end in which these social problems will find their own solution.

In short, Jesus will not be diverted by the demand for a social teaching from the special message of spiritual renewal which He is called to bring. In many of the processes of applied science, there are certain results known as by-products, which are thrown off or precipitated on the way to the special result desired. It may happen that these by-products are of the utmost value; but none the less they are obtained by the way. Such a by-product is the social teaching of Jesus. It was not the end toward which His mission was directed; it came about as He fulfilled His mission. To re-construct the Gospels so as to make them primarily a programme of social reform is to mistake the by-product for the end specifically sought, and in the desire to find a place for Jesus within the modern age, to forfeit that which gives Him His place in all ages.

Again on p. 113 he says:

The teaching of Jesus . . . recognizes that the problem of adjusting social environment must be a new problem with each new age; it concerns itself, therefore, with the making of persons who shall be fit to deal with the environment which each new age in its turn presents.

Our other quotation shall be from the remarkable lectures first delivered by Professor Harnack to the students of the university at Berlin. This is how he speaks of the relation of the Gospel to 'questions of mundane development':

What the Gospel says is this: Whoever you may be, and whatever your position, whether bondman or free, whether fighting or at rest, your real task in life is always the same. There is only *one* relation and *one* idea which you must not violate, and in the face of which all others are only transient wrappings and vain show; to be a child of God and a citizen of His kingdom and to exercise love. How you are to maintain yourself in this life on earth, and in what way you are to serve your neighbour, is left to you and your own liberty of action. This is what the Apostle Paul understood by the Gospel, and I do not believe that he misunderstood it.[1]

It is possible that most of us would wish to modify these statements in some particulars before adopting them as our own; but perhaps the very decisiveness of them may make them the more useful as a corrective of exaggerated representations on the opposite side. The work of the Church is still that of her Master. While far from indifferent to matters which affect material well-being, she may never lose sight of a further goal.

[1] *What is Christianity?* p. 116.

'Man doth not live by bread alone.' The kingdom is 'not of this world'. We want better houses for the people; but we want still more—as it has been aptly put—'better people for the houses'. As Christians we are to welcome most cordially all that is being done to improve the social conditions about us, but we may rightly feel that the fact of such improvement makes it not the less but the more essential that our witness for the spiritual order should be as emphatic and convincing as possible.

It may help us if we remember that the clergy are, not perhaps most liked, but certainly most respected, when it is recognized that they know and do their proper work. It might also be good for us to bear in mind that, whilst men of all occupations greatly value our sympathy, we are not to conclude that they wish for our interference, least of all in cases where an exact understanding of complicated facts and nicely adjusted conditions is indispensable if a just judgment is to be formed.

Hitherto we have been thinking about the danger of secularization as it presents itself in more public ministrations and in connection with certain well-marked tendencies of the present time. Some words must be added upon another aspect of the matter. The peril may approach us on quite different ground, and when we are even less likely to be on our guard against it.

Here we are concerned with a side of the question which is by no means exclusively modern. All writers on the spiritual life have felt it to be necessary to give warnings against the possible effects of a too unreserved mixing in society and a too free participation in its pleasures and pursuits. The need for such counsels is not less now than in former times, and certainly the difficulty both of giving and using them is as great to-day as it can ever have been.

Nothing could be more hopeless than any attempt to draw a line and say, This or that is the limit which may never be overpassed. It would be most undesirable, even were it possible, that any uniformity of type should be established amongst us. It would be a serious thing if the links were to be weakened which have united the English clergy with the general life of society and of the country. Probably the wisest teachers would be the least disposed to lay down rules, and the most ready to concede the largest possible amount of personal liberty.

There can be few of us who would not feel strongly in sympathy with such words as these, spoken some years ago by Dean Vaughan in one of his addresses to younger clergy:

It is a question often asked, and never to be hastily, or perhaps conclusively, answered—How much ought a clergyman to enter into society? There is one answer which is easily given, and which satisfies the spiritual haste and indolence and selfishness of many—Refrain! And there is something in the experience of all persons who would lead a godly life, which responds to that counsel. Who has not come away from a large and promiscuous gathering, from a dinner or an evening party, with a deep consciousness that it has been time wasted, or worse? How natural to draw the inference! For me, at least, this is an unprofitable thing. Others, better men than I am, more devoted, more consistent, may do this thing safely or even with advantage; for me, it is perilous—it is injurious.

Yet let us reflect for a moment what this says. It says that our religion will not bear touching or handling—that it can live and breathe only in solitude; that for us life is not redeemed, only a way is made out of it into another. . . .

It is the experience of many who have not seen their way to this isolation, that when they have gone into society with an earnest prayer for blessing, they have found, ere the evening closed, some opportunity which would otherwise have had no existence, for giving and receiving good—it may be, in the privacy which so often waits upon publicity, the unheard discourse with a casual neighbour whose soul is suddenly opened to one who bears in his face the attribute of 'helper'—they have found reason, thus or otherwise, to rejoice that they had not wrapped themselves in the unsociable mantle of a religion all for itself—they have felt that henceforth they must pray more, and trust more, and expect more, and then God will more largely bless—they will reproach themselves, not others, if they are often frustrated and disappointed in such intercourse—they will feel, nevertheless, that neighbourhood is relationship, and that they have no right to call common or irreligious that interchange of kindliness which God has cleansed.[1]

Side by side with this noble utterance let us set another from an earlier leader of a different school. In a letter written by John Keble to a friend newly ordained we find him saying:

I do not think the glory of God best promoted by a rigid abstinence from amusements, except they be sinful in themselves, or carried to excess, or in some other way ministering occasion to sin. . . . Nor can I well

[1] *Addresses to Young Clergymen*, pp. 111 f.

imagine any greater service to society than is rendered by him, who submits to its common routine, though something wearisome, for this very reason: lest he should offend his neighbours by unnecessary rigour.

Besides, if our neighbours' pleasures be harmless, and we have it in our power to increase them, without breaking any law of God or man, is it quite agreeable to the spirit of Christian charity to refuse to do so? Is it quite agreeable to such passages as 'Rejoice with them that do rejoice'; or to our Saviour's example in working the miracle in Cana, and in submitting to the reproach of beng a man gluttonous and a wine-bibber, rather than offend unthinking sinners by too much preciseness? Is it quite agreeable to the general spirit of the Gospel which directs us, even when we fast, not to be of a sad countenance, and which, next to inculcating the necessity of a thorough inward change, seems anxious to discourage any violent outward one, except when it is a plain duty? . . . Almost every time I look into the New Testament, I feel the more convinced, that the more quietly and calmly one sets about one's duty, and the less one breaks through established customs, always supposing them innocent in themselves, the more nearly does one act according to the great Exemplar there proposed.[1]

We dare not overlook the fact, however, that this liberty of the Gospel has its dangers. All liberty calls for care in the using. Whilst we may fully agree that a policy of ascetic abstention is no true policy, we may nevertheless feel the need of adopting precautions, and even of placing restrictions upon ourselves, lest that which is lawful and beneficial in itself should prove to be an injury to ourselves and to others.

It is not a little significant that Ruskin, when speaking of the personal life of the artist, said that he should be a man who is fitted to move in the best society and who yet 'keeps out of it'! We may easily grasp the meaning of such a remark, even though we may believe that its author did not intend it to be taken quite literally. And, surely, if it be true that the man whose function it is to minister to the higher tastes of his generation has need to be warned against the possible effects upon himself of surroundings and associations which might distract him from a single-eyed pursuit of his ideals; it must be not less true that he also is bound to be most watchful who has been called and set apart that he may witness to realities 'which eye hath not seen, nor ear heard', and the knowledge of which is to be gained

[1] *Letters of Spiritual Counsel*, xii. This was written as early as 1817. It is the more interesting, therefore, to note that the same view is restated in a letter (xiii) bearing date 1860.

and retained by the employment of instincts and faculties far more delicate and liable to be blunted than even the finest perceptions of sense.

If we look for guidance to the example of our Lord, we are struck by the way in which the years and days of His public and social ministry were balanced, so to speak, by spaces of silence and retirement. Our peril lies in the temptation to suppose that we can have much of the one with but scant provision for the other. We need the preparation of solitude if we are to carry influence with us as we pass out into the stream of life.

Moreover a certain skill and wisdom is required if we are to exert our influence with the best effect. We may not assume, as we are perhaps inclined to do, that such moral and spiritual force as we possess will make itself felt independently of any special intention on our part. It is often said that the greatest influence is unconscious influence. Possibly this general statement admits of more qualification than is commonly supposed.

Archbishop Benson, when speaking to one of his junior clergy on the subject of the influence which is to be exercized through social intercourse, warned him that the nature of this influence in any particular instance would greatly depend upon the character of the footing upon which the acquaintance began. There were, he said, in his own case persons with whom it was always easy and natural to speak of the highest topics; and there were others with whom it had never ceased to be difficult to introduce them. The difference he believed to be due to the fact that with the first the higher ground had been taken at the outset, while with the others this had not been so. This experience is one which may furnish matter for reflection to us all.

Certainly the wisest of our laity would pray us to see to it that nothing should induce us to lower our standards of the priestly life. They look to us to help them in ways in which they cannot be helped by one of themselves. They call us 'reverend': it is for us to take care, in all simplicity and with no affectation or assumption, that we are such men as they can highly esteem.

We may learn a great deal by carefully marking the verdicts which are passed upon a ministry that has ended. It is most instructive to observe with what accuracy its main lines and characteristics are usually discerned, and to note how surely the aims and successes are wont to be appraised at their real worth, when for a moment the presence of death seems to have sobered the judgment and made men look with other eyes than those with which they commonly regard the events that are happening about them. At these times even the least religiously minded are able to recognize, and are not slow to reverence, the life-work of the man who has made it his chief business to lift them nearer to God.

It is not easy to say how in a particular instance the danger of which we have been thinking is to be met and overcome. We may not presume to decide for one another. Each man's work will be judged by his Master. Only let us keep in our ears the warnings of that Master as to the salt which loses its savour through a too continuous contact with the earth, and let us remember how again and again He set it before His disciples as their aim that they should be *'in'* the world but *'not of'* it.

Note I

In an Ordination sermon preached in Salisbury Cathedral, in 1876, Dean Church spoke thus to the candidates:

It is much indeed, if there were nothing more, to be members of so illustrious a public body as the clergy of England; to be the inheritors of such a history, to be the guardians of the moral interests of so great a nation. But though you are this, you are more; and woe to you if you forget it. Besides all this, you are the servants and ministers of the Crucified. He on high is your Master, and to Him your account has to be made. It is for His purposes that you are chosen: it is His gifts, His word, His sacraments, that you have to convey to men.

You may, indeed, in a wonderful and increasing measure, be the ministers of the highest earthly blessings to men: but it is the blessings of the world unseen, blessings for weary and endangered souls, blessings for those who have no other hope left them, blessings purchased by the blood of the Eternal Sacrifice, and running on through death into an everlasting life—it is with these that you are specially charged. Do nothing, admit nothing, in the way of employment, in the way of recreation, in what you allow to yourselves, which shall confuse and obscure the thought that yours is a spiritual ministry and stewardship held direct from Jesus Christ, and that you, as He had, have to do with souls.-*Human Life and its Conditions,* pp. 185 f.

Note II

Gentlemen, when a man grows older and sees more deeply into life, he does not find, if he possesses any inner world at all, that he is advanced by the external march of things, by the 'progress of civilisation'. Nay, he feels himself, rather, where he was before, and forced to seek the sources of strength which his forefathers also sought. He is forced to make himself a native of the kingdom of God, the kingdom of the Eternal, the kingdom of Love; and he comes to understand that it was only of this kingdom that Jesus Christ desired to testify, and he is grateful to Him for it.— Adolf Harnack, *What is Christianity?* p. 121.

Chapter 7

Over-Occupation

The danger of which we have been thinking is a most serious one; but there is another against which we have not less need to be on our guard. Indeed, it is probably not too much to say that in it we may find the explanation of the larger part of the failure to attain to the highest ideals, whether in our own lives or in those for whose progress we are responsible. When we trace the indifference, the apathy, the lack of spiritual energy, so noticeable in the world and in the Church, to their ultimate source, we are led to the conclusion that this source is not really hard to discover, and that it admits of being described in language which is perfectly plain. The symptoms are simply those of exhaustion; and the exhaustion is due to the fact that the vital powers, interests, and sympathies have been too constantly stimulated and too indiscriminately drawn upon.

To take an illustration. A great deal of the inability to believe, and the indisposition to make the efforts required by religion, which is often accounted for as the effect of the unsettlement produced by scientific thought, should in all probability be regarded as traceable to this cause of which we are now to speak.

There are some brave, clear words written by Dr Pritchard, the Oxford professor, on this matter which deserve to be carefully noted and remembered. In answer to the question, 'Is it true that the pursuit of Science has any inherent tendency towards religious scepticism?' he gave it as his firm conviction that, 'It is *preoccupation of mind*, rather than science, which is, and ever has been, the prolific parent of scepticism and of indifference in religion'; and he went on to ask, 'Are not the preoccupations of high position, the preoccupations of ambition, of literature, of money-getting and of money-spending, of conceit, of sensual habits, and even of idleness, at least as unfriendly to the hearty acceptance of the Christian revelation, as are the preoccupations of scientific pursuits?'[1]

The same thing, in effect, was said in a no less striking way by R. H. Hutton, the editor of the *Spectator*. He was deploring 'the meagre amount of life which remains to be thrown into the search for spiritual truth after all the other excitements of life have been provided for'. 'There is now,' he insisted, 'no adequate economy of human strength for the higher objects of life, too much a great deal being lavished on its petty interests.' 'If men come to Christ with exhausted natures they will never know what there is in Him. . . . No doubt Christianity offers a new life of its own, and an inexhaustible spring of that life; but it offers it only to those who can give a life for a life, who can give up the whole mind and heart, that a new mind and a new heart may be substituted for them.' 'A generation, of which the most impressive characteristic is its spiritual fatigue, will never be truly Christian till it can husband its energy better, and consent to forego many petty interests that it may not forego the religion of the Cross.'[2]

These testimonies are of great value, coming as they do from men of our own time who have had unusual opportunities of forming a judgment as to the temper of their age. But we may go back to much earlier and higher authority, and find the same moral enforced by One who spoke for human nature in every age.

It is more than likely that already there has flashed upon our memories the recollection of our Lord's parable of the sower and the seed. Of all the parables none is more calculated to arrest the attention of those who to-day are seeking guidance as to the best means of making progress in spiritual life. None certainly is more surprisingly in line with the direction taken by the thinking just quoted, or more closely in touch with our needs and our difficulties.

Religion, as it is set forth in this parable, is a strangely simple thing. Its beginnings are from God. Good influences, impressions, suggestions, inspirations, come to us—as the terms in

---

[1] *Occasional Thoughts of an Astronomer on Nature and Revelation*, pp. 10 f.
[2] See the article reprinted in *Aspects of Religious and Scientific Thought*, pp. 21 f.

which we describe them imply—from a source outside and above ourselves. They are as *seeds* scattered upon the soil of our nature. If we may venture upon a simple retranslation, which would bring the old language almost startlingly into accord with our modes of thought and expression, we might say that they are *germs* with which the spiritual atmosphere about us is charged.

But the fact that they come to us is only half the truth. If it is certain that 'we do not make our thoughts', it is equally certain that 'they grow in us'. They come to us, and they become part of us conditioned by their association with us, strengthening with our strength and developing with our development. They grow in us into convictions, into actions, into habits, into character, into destiny. Thus it is that the seed is 'the word of the kingdom', carrying with it the potentiality and the promise of all that is highest in human life, both here and hereafter.

This, which is the general teaching of the parable, is the preparation for the particular lessons which follow. The religious life has its beginnings from God. Its progress is largely dependent upon ourselves. There are accordingly conditions which must be fulfilled by us, in proportion to the fulfilment of which will be the growth unto perfection. These conditions, as we have them stated, are of the most elementary kind.

In the first place, the seed must get *in*; it must meet with a welcome, and be permitted to win an entrance into mind and heart. In the next place, it must get *down*; it must be laid hold of by the deeper parts of the nature, until it has penetrated the conscience and taken its place among the principles which shape the thoughts and guide the will. Lastly, it must get *room*. Space must be secured for it, so that it shall not be overshadowed and starved by any rival growths. The other conditions might be complied with, and yet the results be sadly disappointing, if this final condition were to remain unfulfilled.

It is the insistence upon this final condition that brings us face to face with the danger against which we have such special need to be on our watch to-day. Here, from the lips of our Lord Himself, is the very warning which the writers whom we have previously quoted urged us to consider. How much do we not owe to the form in which His lesson is conveyed? How easy it is to see the force of truth thus luminously illustrated. The facts are there all obvious before our eyes. The soil of our being can supply the needed sustenance to but a limited number of growths. The attempt to include more than can be healthily maintained must prove injurious to them all; and, in the stress of the competition, the most delicate and sensitive of the seedlings will naturally fare the worst.

How plain then is our duty when we are called upon to advise. When persons come to us and tell us, as they continually do, that their faith and hope have become weakened and dim, and that their hold upon the unseen is feeble and faltering; when they complain that it is only with the greatest difficulty that they can give their attention for any length of time to spiritual things, while all other interests seem to to have more power to occupy their thoughts and enlist their sympathies, it ought not to be difficult for us to see what course we should follow.

In a large majority of such cases the right prescription is a a simple one. We have but to say:

Your life is too crowded, you have allowed too many interests to enter in and absorb your vital strength; too many plants are struggling for existence in the garden of your nature. It is simply another case of 'no room to live'. You will have to thin out. You must see to it that the good seed gets its proper chance. Reduce the number of excitements and engrossments, make more free spaces for stillness and quiet thought, and see if you do not soon begin to feel the gain in the strengthening of what is best in your life.'

But here, as always, before we can hope to get our counsel attended to, we must have gained the wisdom and the courage to apply it to ourselves. We may not suppose that we need it less than others. It is quite likely that we need it more. We have indeed temptations to yield to distractions which would draw us away from higher tasks into activities which lie outside our proper sphere. Of these we have spoken in the previous chapter. In regard to these, as has been admitted, the line is not to be easily drawn; but the difficulty of discrimination becomes immensely increased when the selection of interests and occupations has to be attempted, not without, but within the departments for which we are directly responsible.

How familiar the problem sounds as we begin to describe it! Work, as ever, has resulted in more work. The demands upon us have gone on increasing. Engagements thicken. There are people to be visited, services to be taken, sermons and addresses to be prepared, meetings to be attended, appeals to be issued, letters to be answered. And there is 'no time', as we say, for careful study, for devotional reading, for the daily offices, or for patient intercession. A general restlessness has entered the life, we find it increasingly difficult to be still; and with it all the growth of the spirit is retarded. Though many things are done, we are painfully aware that but little is really accomplished.

No doubt a certain amount of ordering and regulating would in many instances do much to remedy the evil. Even to write down on a slip of paper at the beginning of the day an outline of the work to be attempted in it, might be of considerable service in securing reasonable arrangement and consequent economy of strength, not to speak of the relief from the strain of a perpetual uncertainty as to what should be undertaken next.

But with some of us a treatment of a more drastic sort is required. Before regulation can usefully begin there must be a change which is tantamount to revolution. We must determine that, whatever happens, it shall be 'First things first'. The highest interests must have the foremost place in our lives. The spirit must be secured its close times for uninterrupted communing with the sources of its strength. The hour of meditation must be protected as men were wont to guard the well in the fortress. The mind must be braced and refreshed by intercourse with the best thought of the present and the past. And for the rest, the watchword must be *multum non multa*. We must simply decline, with whatever sorrow, to undertake more things than we can hope to do well.

'Mastery,' said Lord Acton, in his inaugural lecture at Cambridge, 'is acquired by resolved limitation.'

Dr Liddon used to tell how, at the outset of his ministerial career, when, as he put it, he 'was in danger of becoming a popular preacher', he had received from Dr Pusey a piece of advice which had been to him of the utmost value. It was this: 'Limit your work.'

It may sound paradoxical to say, Limit your work, that you may extend your influence; but the principle involved is a true one. It is quality and not quantity that tells. The work done by the worker in a healthful condition of mind and spirit, calmed and sustained by the consciousness of the Divine approval and guidance, which inevitably disappears in an atmosphere of hurry and bustle, is the work that is really fruitful of results that remain.

Let it not be imagined that such limitation of work will open the door to idleness. It would be more true to say that it is the most certain way of deliverance from it. Possibly, if the truth were known, it would be seen that much of the activity of to-day is in reality the effect of indolence. The line of least resistance is that which we are naturally disposed to take. We find it much easier to employ our bodily powers than to exert our intellectual faculties; and most of all do we shrink from the effort involved in the use of our souls. How many of us who are perpetually saying that we have 'no time' to think, or to pray, would be more likely to do either if we were set down in the depths of the country? Verily there is an indolence which disguises itself from itself under the cloak of untiring activity.

Nor need we be greatly afraid lest such a limitation of work—perhaps we should rather say of works—should prove to be prejudicial to our parishes. Many a parish would be greatly the gainer if its clergy were less ready, and indeed eager, to do everything themselves.

We are continually being told of the slowness with which lay help is developed amongst us; and, as often as not, in the same breath it is said that the clergy are having the life crushed out of them by persistent overwork. The fault may in a measure be that of the laity, but must we not acknowledge that in a large number of instances it has been the clergy themselves who have been chiefly to blame?

How many a time it would have been good if some one could have gone to the over-occupied parish priest, who was on his feet rushing hither and thither from morning to night, and said:

Brother, you forget that there is such a thing as 'the sacred principle of delegation'. It is sometimes true to say, If you want a thing well done, don't do it yourself! It may cost you not a little to train some one else to do it, and there is a certain amount of distress in seeing the thing done not exactly as you would have done it: but by giving the work to another you would summon fresh powers into action, powers which in all probability would continue to operate long after you are gone. If you go on as you are going, you will be inflicting a serious wrong upon others, as well as an injury upon yourself.

Who does not know of cases where the weak health of a vicar has actually proved to have been a blessing in disguise? The people have rallied to help him by undertaking a score of things which, had he been more robust, he would probably have thought it easiest to do for himself. The result has been that new interests have entered their lives, and given a new direction to their thoughts and energies; while he has become, far more effectively than might otherwise have been possible, the head and the heart of the parochial organization.

Would indeed that we had all of us more courage to believe that whatever makes a clergyman a more vitally powerful man, capable of being and doing his very best, must ultimately tend to the highest well-being of his parish. If we really believed this, we should be more alive than we are to the danger of being much occupied in 'many things'; and should realize that no array of statistics to be tabulated in a yearbook can compensate for the lack of the 'one thing needful'—the growth and development of personal spiritual life.

Note

Since writing the above I have met with a valuable corroboration of what I have ventured to say by Sir John R. Seeley, formerly Professor of Modern History at Cambridge.

Not only in the Church, [he maintained] but among the teaching class at the Universities and in school, as idleness was the besetting sin of the last age, industry is the besetting sin of the present; or, more correctly, the idleness has been succeeded by a merely external and superficial industry. Our conversion seems to have begun not at the heart but at the extremities. The hands and feet have thrown off their listlessness and move to and fro indefatigably; the tongue, throat, and lungs tax themselves prodigiously; but the change will be more in form than in substance till it penetrates to the brain and will. In all the professions a man's first duty now is to renounce the ambition of becoming distinguished for activity; the temptation chiefly to be avoided is that of undertaking more than he can do in first-rate style.

The quality of work must be improved, and for that end, if necessary, the quantity reduced. A higher and calmer sort of activity must be arrived at—economy in energy, expenditure without waste, zeal without haste.—*Lectures and Essays*, 'The Church as a Teacher of Morality', pp. 282 f.

Chapter 8

Depression

Great are the blessings, and great is the power of cheerfulness. 'Give me the man,' wrote Carlyle, 'who sings at his work.'

If it be the case, and none of us would be likely to question it, that a happy contentment adds charm and value to all other sorts of labour, such a disposition is specially to be desired in the case of those who are appointed to minister in holy things. If it be true, as Faber has declared, that 'melancholy in a creature is a kind of injurious reflection upon the Creator', how prejudicial must habitual sadness be on the part of men whose mission it is to witness for God and to win others to serve Him? Could anything be more calculated to counteract the effect of their message than an impression that they are themselves disappointed, or even embittered, by their experiences of life? They of all men should, in the well-known phrase of the good Bishop Hackett, 'serve God and be cheerful.'

So much we should all of us find it easy to say; yet, at the same time, we might rightly feel that the statement of the case would scarcely be complete if left to stand in this unqualified shape. There is need to distinguish, and to define our meaning more carefully, for while we may be ready enough to allow that a cheerful bearing is, as a rule, most attractive, and of the greatest assistance in commending the Gospel of glad tidings, there are other aspects of the matter which ought not to be ignored. We may assent to the general proposition that it is desirable to avoid the feeling and appearance of sadness as we go about our work, and yet we may have considerable doubt as to how far it is always possible to do this; and further still, as to whether it can, under all circumstances, be right to attempt it.

Was there not truth, as well as cleverness, in the reply of the bishop who had been posed by a notorious sceptic with the question, 'Why is it that all the Christians that I meet are so melancholy?' Said the bishop, 'The sight of you, Mr.—, would make any Christian melancholy.'

Had not the author of the once popular *Proverbial Philosophy* some reason on his side when he wrote, 'No man can look on the world, and be both happy and good'? Is there not a happiness which is largely the result of shallowness?

Dare we proceed on the assumption that to a Christian believer this life of ours presents no difficulties of the graver sort? Would it not, on the contrary, be more true to maintain that to a Christian the disorders and enigmas of the world are perplexing and embarrassing just in proportion as his heart is tender, and his zeal for the Divine honour is great?

Is it not the fact that the idealist—be he artist, or poet, or prophet—by the very constitution of his nature, is more liable to alternations and revulsions of feeling than are others whose gifts are of a different order? If he has his hill-top moments of vision, he has also his descents into the shadows. He is haunted by conceptions of beauty, or goodness, or truth, which he imperfectly apprehends, and yet more imperfectly expresses; and the sense of his failure brings with it often the very keenest distress. But is it not a noble pain? Is there not a blessedness which belongs to those who 'mourn', and to those who experience the 'hunger and thirst' of the spirit?

Was it not the 'Man of Sorrows' who went about doing good as none other ever did? And are we not constantly saying that suffering is that which equips and qualifies for the most difficult tasks; that it is only through suffering that we can hope to gain the delicacy of sympathy which is essential to those who are to minister to the wounded of heart and of soul?

Clearly then, as we said, there is need to distinguish. We may not decide offhand that all sadness is a wrong or an unprofitable sadness. There is a Christian distress at the sight of the world as it is; a sorrow which is the evidence not of death in the soul, but of life. Such a distress, we may even make bold to affirm, so far from repelling those who witness it, has in it a strange power to arrest men's attention, and to win them to seriousness of thought and endeavour.

We must be careful not to cast any slight upon the noble and unselfish sorrow which has such good reasons to give for itself, and which has seldom been entirely absent from the lives of the greatest thinkers and workers. Such sorrow has in it nothing of the bitterness of despair; indeed, not the least wonderful thing about it is, that it is wont to be accompanied by a deep and mysterious joy.

It is not then of this sorrow that we are to think as we proceed to consider the last of the dangers which we shall attempt to describe. There is a sadness of very different origin and character, which has no such purifying or arresting power. It arises not from the presence, but from the absence of ideals. It owes nothing of its poignancy to solicitude for the Divine honour. It contributes nothing that can be of value to the service of man. Such is the sadness which is properly described as *depression*.

The symptoms of it are unhappily too familiar to us all. It shows itself in moodiness and indisposition for effort, in a morbid self-consciousness and weary dissatisfaction with persons and circumstances.

Heaviness, gloom, coldness, sullenness, distaste and desultory sloth in work and prayer, joylessness, and thanklessness—do we not know something of the threatenings, at least, of a mood in which these meet? The mood of days . . . when, as one has said, 'everything that everybody does seems inopportune and out of good taste'; days when the things that are true and honest, just and pure, lovely and of good report, seem to have lost all loveliness and glow and charm of hue, and look as dismal as a flat country in the drizzling mist of an east wind; days when we might be cynical if we had a little more energy in us; when all enthusiasm and confidence of hope, all sense of a Divine impulse, flags out of our work; when the schemes which we have begun look stale and poor and unattractive as the scenery of an empty stage by daylight; days when there is nothing that we *like* to do—when without anything to complain of, nothing stirs so readily in us as complaint.[1]

Some of us are, of course, more disposed by temperament to fall into depression than others, but there can be few of us who have not cause to dread the miseries of it. We can scarcely take too serious a view of the danger, and of our responsibility in regard to it.

[1] Bishop Paget, *The Spirit of Discipline*, pp. 59 f.

What we may hope to be able to say about precautions and remedies will probably seem, when it is written down, to be bald and inadequate; but nevertheless it will be worth while to gather together some of the counsels and suggestions which have been offered from time to time, and which we should probably think it only natural to offer, if the advice were intended for others rather than for ourselves.

To begin, then, with ordinary and elementary considerations that bear upon the subject. A great deal depends simply upon *bodily* health. We who labour with our brains have more need to concern ourselves about principles and rules of diet than those have who work with their hands. It may make a great difference, too, whether the study in which we do our thinking is a room that gets a fair share of the sunshine. Then it must be remembered that the clergy have no more right than others to imagine that they can go on ignoring that necessity of our nature which underlies the appointment of one day's rest in seven, and expect to escape with impunity. It is extremely difficult to secure the weekly break, and we shall only succeed in doing it if we regard the duty as one which we owe to those for whom we work as much as to ourselves.

Passing to *intellectual* conditions, we cannot shut our eyes to the fact that the mind has its needs no less than the body. It also demands recreation and reinvigoration. With some of us the relief and renewal are most successfully sought in one way, with some in another. Congenial social intercourse, a good novel, or it may be a good play, afford what is evidently the best means of healthful unbending to many; while those who are differently constituted, are equally the better for the tonic effect of a really stiff book on some subject the furtherest removed from any which ordinarily occupies their thoughts.

For all of us it would seem to be essential that we should from time to time withdraw from our work for the sake of our work. We note how the artist at intervals steps back from his canvas, that he may gain a broader and juster impression of what he is about. Even so it is of the greatest importance that the parish priest should occasionally step back from his task and its immediate surroundings. Seen from the distance things stand out in truer proportions. Troubles and difficulties, for instance, which close at hand fill the entire horizon, wear a quite altered aspect if looked at from an outside standpoint from which it is possible to measure their real significance, or insignificance, in relation to the work as a whole. When, moreover, the withdrawal has been combined with something of the nature of a Retreat, in which the worker not only steps back but rises up and attains to a fresh vision of what he and his fellows are doing from the point of view of the Master Artist under whom he and they are engaged, how delightful the refreshment may be; and with what added insight and courage and patience he may go down from the mount to toil on at the bit of the great design with which he has been entrusted.

Questions of money have not a little to do with freedom of mind. It may seem commonplace to insist upon the necessity of keeping accounts, and of avoiding debt, and of living within the limits of income whatever the income may be; yet failure in these duties must mean misery, and may mean disaster. No men have more cause than the clergy to believe in the truth of the promise that to those who 'seek first the kingdom' all things necessary for life and for godliness shall 'be added'; but neither exegesis nor experience affords any grounds for supposing that the fulfilment of that promise is to be expected where, through carelessness, in the ordinary meaning of the word, the common precautions of foresight and prudence have been neglected.

It is well that we should have it impressed upon us that the disciplined life is the healthy life. Great is the peace of those who have trained themselves into the love of order and law. Much of the feeling of weakness and unsatisfactoriness, which is the torment of many, is to be traced to nothing else than a want of method and of the most ordinary self-control.

Such are some of the observations which first suggest themselves in connection with this subject of depression. We enter upon much less sure ground when we proceed to deal with the matter not so much as a physical failing, or an intellectual weakness, but as a *spiritual* temptation.

There can be no question at all that it is to be so regarded and treated. As the danger of secularization may be said to have its ultimate source in the power of the world to lower to its own levels the standards and aspirations of the religious life; and as the danger of over-occupation can be traced to the desire of the flesh to substitute its own activities for those of the spirit: so, on a final analysis, we are driven to the conclusion that the danger of depression derives its chief terrors for us from the fact that it is a most fatally successful snare of the devil.

There is One from whom we draw our thoughts of hope: even so there is one principal author of discouragement and despair. Many and subtle are the devices by which he seeks to entice us from the light, that he may fill our souls with gloom. If we are to escape them we must stand continually on our guard against them.

Especially are we bound to keep watch over our thoughts and desires. If we are to be preserved from much misery, we must watch our ambitions. The loftier we pitch these the better. They can work us nothing but good when they rise to the longing that we may attain to our best, and be allowed to do something here and hereafter to forward the great purposes of God. They tend to be mischievous so soon as they become bound up with the craving for immediate recognition and the desire for a merely personal reward. That way lies the possibility of all manner of disappointment and vexation.

Closely allied to the pride of a false ambition is the pride of a wrong dependence upon our own powers. It has been truly said, and we shall do well to ponder the remark, that 'despondency is self-confidence which has failed.'

Then, too, we must jealously guard our satisfactions. Our eyes must be ever unto the hills from whence cometh our strength. The heart that tries to sustain itself upon human commendation will discover with bitterness that the demand will ever increase, while at the same time the sense of emptiness will be more and more painfully felt. 'Whosoever drinketh of this water shall thirst again.' If we are wise, we shall taste the cup of human praise with something of fear and trembling. There is no more certain cause of depression than the accepting of lower satisfactions. The higher may seem hard to reach, and may at first have less power to stir and inspire the heart, but the effect of them grows with experience, and their glow is the glow of health and not the flush of excitement. 'At Thy right hand there are pleasures for evermore.'

Again, if we are to escape unnecessary distress, we shall keep most diligent watch upon our criticisms. We little realize how potent an enemy to peace is the habit of judging our brethren. Criticisms, like curses, 'come home to roost'. The critical spirit inevitably grows to be morbidly self-conscious and sensitive. So certain is it that, 'With what measure ye mete, it shall be measured to you again.'

For the rest there is the supreme remedy of humble faith in God and patient acceptance of His appointment. For the believer in the Cross of Christ difficulties may and do remain in the world as he sees it. He cannot presume to suppose that he possesses the final clue to the problem of Infinite Wisdom. He works on in the assurance that what he knows not now he will know hereafter. If God has not fully shown him His mind, He has done what is better—He has shown him His heart; for 'There is no sacrifice that God has not made for man'! To one who believes this difficulties may remain, but doubt has gone for ever.

We can trust Him wholly with His world. We can trust Him with ourselves. We are sure that He cares far more to make the best of us, and to do the most through us, than we have ever cared ourselves. He is ever trying to make us understand that He yearns to be to us more than aught in the universe besides. That He really wants us, and needs us, is the wonder and strength of our life.

To those with whom these are the chief certainties of existence there may indeed come hours of darkness and mysterious trial, assaults of the evil one, and chastisements for sins that are past: but behind all a light is shining from before which, sooner or later, the clouds must break and the shadows must flee away.

Note

No treatment of the subject of ministerial depression is more full of pathos and suggestiveness than that which is to be found in a sermon by F. W. Robertson upon the despondency of Elijah (*Sermons*, ii. pp. 73 f.). Every word comes pulsing from the inmost heart of the speaker. A few sentences may give an impression of its general purport, but it should be carefully studied as a whole.

We are fearfully and wonderfully made. Of that constitution, which in our ignorance we call union of soul and body, we know little respecting what is cause and what is effect. We would fain believe that the mind has power over the body, but it is just as true that the body rules the mind. Causes apparently the most trivial: a heated room—want of exercise—a sunless day—a northern aspect—will make all the difference between happiness and unhappiness, between faith and doubt, between courage and indecision. . . .

What greater minds like Elijah's have felt intensely, all we have felt in our own degree. Not one of us but what has felt his heart aching for want of sympathy. We have had our lonely hours, our days of disappointment, and our moments of hopelessness—times when our highest feelings have been misunderstood, and our purest met with ridicule. Days when our heavy secret was lying unshared, like ice upon the heart. And then the spirit gives way: we have wished that all were over—that we could lie down tired, and rest like the children, from life—that the hour was come when we could put down the extinguisher on the lamp, and feel the last grand rush of darkness on the spirit.

After tracing with extraordinary insight the Divine treatment of Elijah's case by the administration of 'food, rest, and exercise', 'by the healing influences of nature', by 'work to be done', and by 'the assurance of victory', the preacher concludes:

Remember the power of *indirect* influences: those which distil from a life, not from a sudden, brilliant effort. The former never fail: the latter often. There is good done of which we can never predict the when or where. . . . Get below appearances, below glitter and show. Plant your foot upon reality. Not in the jubilee of the myriads on Carmel, but in the humble silence of the hearts of the seven thousand, lay the proof that Elijah had not lived in vain.

Postscript

No attempt has been made in these pages to disguise the fact that the life of the Christian, and particularly of the clergy, is a difficult one. 'Difficulty', as we saw, is the central watchword of the three in the Exhortation of the Ordinal. The day has certainly gone, if ever there was such a day, when men might persuade themselves that by entering into Holy Orders they were securing an agreeable and not very arduous career. From the clergy more than from any other workers is expected self-sacrifice in devotion to their work. None of us would complain that this is so. We are grateful for the support which we receive when those about us demand from us that we should be our best. We feel that our own standards ought to be even higher than theirs for us.

After all, life in this world is only a choice of difficulties. If we avoid them in one direction it is but to meet them in another. It will cost us much to be true to our vocation, but the penalty will be greater if we are not. It is 'hard to be a Christian', but it is harder *not* to be! When those who have once seen the vision and 'tasted the heavenly gift' draw back, they invite experiences compared with which the trials of the saint are light and sweet. The really 'hard' thing is to 'kick against the pricks'. 'The way of transgressors is hard.'

We dare not then be daunted by the difficulties before us. There is One who knows them all, and who is ready to meet them with us. 'Faithful is He that calleth, who also will do it.' What is wanted on our part is patience and hope. We must 'do the next best thing', set our foot on the next rung of the ladder, however elementary or unattractive the duty may seem. We must remember, as we have said already, that every true effort is sure to be repaid. We must be willing to learn by our failures. Perhaps most of all, we must be resolute in putting from us the ignoble and cowardly suggestion, 'If only I might begin somewhere else, and make a new start under fresh conditions, I could be this or the other.' Rather let us thank God, if we have done badly where we are, that He still leaves us the opportunity of making a reparation before the eyes of those who have been wronged by our negligence.

We can always begin again, if we are humble and put our confidence in God. It will not be easy, but it is possible. We may not ask for more.